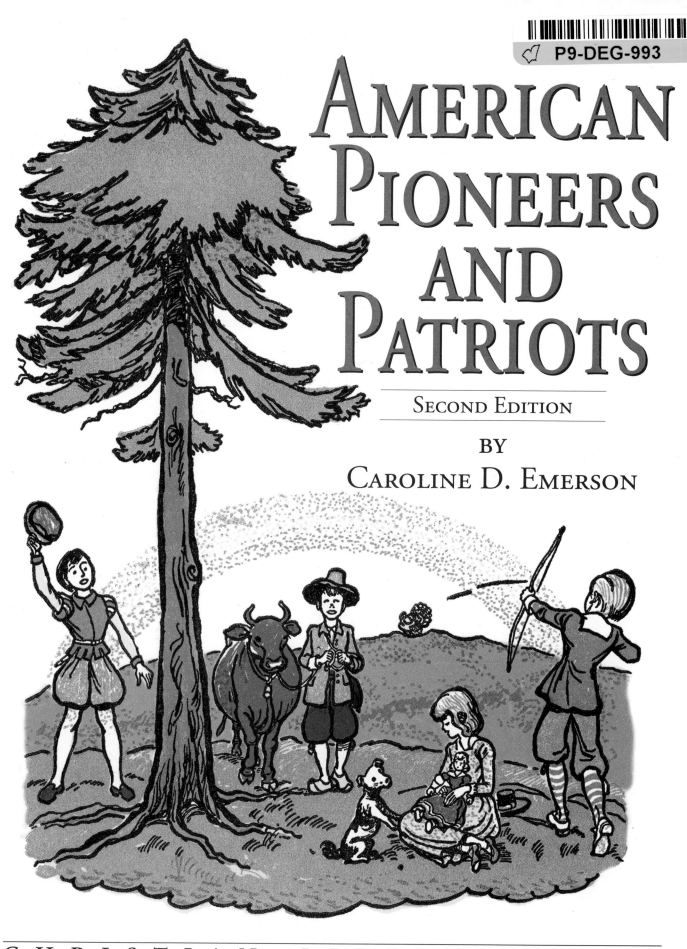

AMERICAN PIONEERS AND PATRIOTS

SECOND EDITION

BY

CAROLINE D. EMERSON

CHRISTIAN LIBERTY PRESS
ARLINGTON HEIGHTS, ILLINOIS

2002 Printing

printed by

Christian Liberty Press
502 West Euclid Avenue
Arlington Heights, Illinois 60004
www.christianlibertypress.com

Editor:
Michael J. McHugh

Graphics:
William Sharp, Eric Bristley, Edward J. Shewan

Design:
Bob Fine

Proofreading:
Diane Olson, Lars Johnson

Ad maiorem

Dei gloriam

Christian Liberty Press
502 West Euclid Avenue
Arlington Heights, Illinois 60004
www.christianlibertypress.com

ISBN 1-930367-82-1

Printed in the United States of America

Foreword

The stories that follow will present young students with a uniquely rewarding study of early American history and culture. Young people will be exposed to more than a dry, narrow study of major political and military events from the annals of our country's history. They will learn about the growth and development of the United States from the perspective of those who lived through this time.

A true study of history is, in many respects, a study of people. Sometimes it seems as though grown-up people have more than their fair share of exciting adventures. This seems especially true when we read about the days of old in America. Grown men like Captain John Smith had the fun of landing in Jamestown, and Daniel Boone had the joy of cutting a trail west through the forest. These men and other pioneers built the first houses. They hunted and trapped animals. They were the ones who had adventures with the Indians.

However, the grown people had only half of the adventures. Families founded our country, and families meant boys and girls. These early American families were large, and the young people counted for a great deal. The boys and girls had more than their fair share of hard work to do. They had their share of danger and risks, too. There were whole families that went west across our country in covered wagons. That meant crossing deep rivers and hot, dry wastelands. It meant walking, walking, walking, for hundreds and hundreds of miles. It meant, perhaps, being killed by Indians.

This book is made up of stories about boys and girls who lived in different places and times in our country. They are exciting stories. It is important, however, to remember that these fictional stories represent real boys and girls who lived during this time in history.

The boys in pioneer days cut down the forests and burned the brush. They did their share in planting the land and reaping the crops. They also took care of the cows and pigs and sheep. And they hunted with their fathers. In addition, the girls learned to spin and sew and bake. Girls learned to shoot, too. They learned to stand by their fathers and brothers and load the old-fashioned guns when Indians attacked.

It was exciting to be a boy or girl in those days, but it is just as exciting to be young today. In fact, it is more exciting. Pedro, who came to Florida in a sailing ship, had never seen a train or an airplane. Molly Harris, the little girl in this book who went over the Wilderness Trail to Kentucky, had never seen a city, an automobile, or a movie. Today boys and girls can see more, hear more, learn more, and do more than in the days of the pioneers. Only by studying the past can young people realize how greatly God has chosen to bless our beloved country. Children in America too often take their modern conveniences for granted.

It is just as important for young people to be effective today, as they were in early America. The more we know, the more useful we can be. The more we learn, the more we can help make our country a better place in which to live. These stories help children to understand that God's gifts of faith, courage, and determination are what transformed our early pioneers into patriots.

Michael J. McHugh

— Contents —

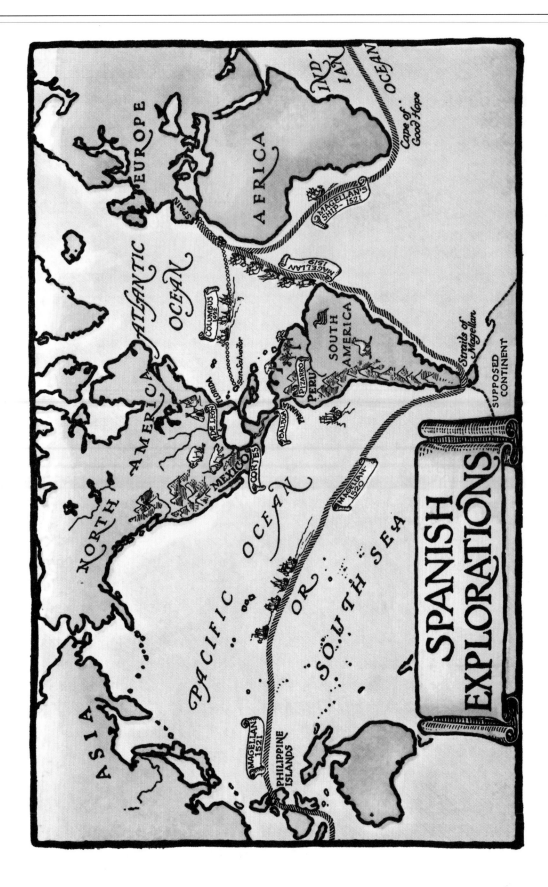

First Pioneers

A STORY OF PIONEER CHILDREN FROM SPAIN

Pioneers are people who come to a new land to make new homes. Who were the first pioneers to come to this great land of ours?

The Indians came first. For more than two thousand years, Indians were the only people living here. Indian children were the first pioneer children in America.

Where did the Indians come from? We do not know. We can only guess. Some Indians may have come from Asia. They probably built log rafts or wooden boats and sailed from one small island to the next. So, little by little, they came to America.

Then, about a thousand years ago, the first white men came across the Atlantic Ocean. They were called Vikings. They found a great land covered with forests. They saw Indians. But they did not stay here. They sailed home.

Next came a man from Spain. His name was Columbus. He had three ships under his control. The ships were called the *Nina,* the *Pinta,* and the *Santa Maria.* But Columbus did not stay in this new land. He went back to Spain.

Years later, more Spanish settlers came and began to build homes. In the year 1565, thirty-four ships sailed from Spain. They carried more than two thousand people. They were going to start a town in Florida.

What was it like crossing the ocean to Florida in 1565? There were no swift ocean-going ships in those days. There were only sailing ships. Wind blew against the sails to push the ships along.

When no wind blew, these ships were helpless. They had no engines. Without the wind, they could not move.

There were no electric lights on the ships. There were no freezers. In fact, there were no stoves on which to cook.

Today an ocean liner can cross the Atlantic Ocean in five days. An airplane can fly across in less than a day.

In 1565, there were no airplanes. There were no telephones. There were no radios or televisions. No one knew what might happen when a ship started off. The trip took several months. Sometimes ships were wrecked and never came to shore.

What was it like crossing the ocean to Florida in 1565? The next story will tell you.

Pedro and Catalina

Chapter 1
Leaving Spain

Pedro was nine years old. He could not read or write, but few people could in 1565. He could ride a horse, and he was learning to use a small sword. Already he owned a sharp hunting knife.

Catalina was Pedro's sister. She was only seven, but she wore a long, full skirt that nearly touched the floor. She, too, could not read or write. When she added, she counted on her fingers. But she could sew and spin thread. She could sing and dance. Everyone in the village knew and liked her.

Pedro and Catalina and their father and mother were leaving Spain. They were leaving the village where Pedro and Catalina had been born and where they had always lived. They were to sail across the sea in a ship. There had been days and nights of talking and planning. Catalina's mother had wept. It was sad to leave one's old home!

The house had been sold. The pans and kettles had been packed. Clothes and blankets were folded in the big chest. The feather bed was tied up in a roll. Mother ran out to her garden for a last look. She had seeds from the orange and fig trees. She wanted to plant them in her garden in the New World.

"We must not forget anything!" she cried. "There will be no shops in the forest. Pedro cannot run back across the ocean for something we forget."

Then, at last, the family stood on the deck of the ship that was to carry them across the ocean. Mother and Catalina had nearly cried their eyes out saying good-bye to their friends, but Pedro was too excited to cry. He almost forgot to help his father carry the big chest on board. He wanted to see everything.

The harbor was a busy place that

summer day. Many ships were ready to sail. More than two thousand people were starting for Florida. From each ship flew huge silken flags. The sea gulls flew screaming through the air.

"Perhaps we shall find gold in the new land," said Pedro's father. "Perhaps we shall all grow rich."

"More likely, we shall all be shipwrecked!" cried Pedro's mother. "Perhaps my precious children will be pulled from the water by painted Indians and made into slaves!"

Catalina stared at her mother in fear, but Pedro was not afraid. He put his hand on the knife he wore at his belt. He was ready for any adventure. He wanted to see the Indians.

Suddenly the ship shook with the roar of cannon. Catalina clapped her hands to her ears, but Pedro liked the noise. Trumpets sounded and drums beat. A loud cheer went up. The sails had been raised against the blue sky. The fresh salt breeze filled them.

Pedro shouted as loudly as he could, but Catalina held her mother's hand tightly. Then something happened that surprised them both. The deck beneath their feet began slowly to rise and fall. They had left the smooth water of the harbor. The waves were tossing the ship up and down. It was headed for the open sea. The trip had begun.

Pedro and Catalina watched the houses and trees on shore grow smaller and smaller. Then the fair land of Spain was only a dark line. The blue sea stretched ahead.

"We must find the cabin," said their mother. "Where do we go? What do we do?

We must find our things. We must find bunks to sleep on." It all seemed very strange.

She hurried them from the bright sunlight into the dim cabin. It seemed hot and crowded in there. It was filled with people and chests. People tumbled over boxes and bumped into each other.

"I wish this ship would stay still," said Catalina.

"It won't do that, not even for the King of Spain himself," laughed a woman.

Pedro unfastened a bundle for his mother. Catalina helped spread blankets on the wooden bunks. Each family had brought its own blankets and dishes. There was little space to put things. People were beginning to complain. Catalina did not like the hot and sticky air. Her father took her and Pedro out on deck.

The fresh salt breeze made Pedro hungry. M-m-m, the good smell of food! The cook had a great iron kettle hanging over a fire that blazed in a big box of sand on the deck. There were dried peas and salt

The ships rose and fell on the waves. The sun had almost set. It was time for the evening prayer and hymn.

"Listen!" whispered Catalina softly to her mother. Across the waves came the sound of other voices, on the other ships, singing the same hymn. Over a thousand voices joined in the song.

The sun dropped big and red into the water. People started for the cabin. That first night Pedro and Catalina found the wooden bunks hard. They tossed and turned. The two lanterns, with candles burning in them, swung back and forth from the low ceiling of the cabin. They sent strange shadows dancing across the walls.

meat boiling together. Pedro ran back to his mother for bowls. The cook filled one for him and one for Catalina. The hot food tasted good. Afterwards, mother brought them nuts and raisins. Pedro and Catalina stood by the rail eating. The sun was setting.

There was no clock aboard. Every half hour, a boy turned the sand glass. The sand ran slowly through a little hole. It took just half an hour. Then the glass must be turned over. As the boy turned the glass, he sang out the time for all to hear:

Just as the children fell asleep at last, they heard the timekeeper call out the hour:

God give us a good night and good sailing! ❏

One glass is gone and now another turneth,
More will run through, if our God willeth!

Chapter 2
Storm at Sea

At first, the weather was fair, so the children played on deck. Pedro found a boy his own age. His name was Martin. Pedro showed Martin his knife. Catalina also made a pet of the ship's cat. It had four kittens.

During the day, the boys listened to an old sailor who had already been to this new land called Florida. He told them tales of Indians in the strange land.

"They're a great sight, those Indian chiefs," said the old man. "They have tall feathers in their hair, and they are painted from head to foot."

"Did you ever go hunting with the Indi-ans?" asked the boys eagerly.

"We once watched them hunt alliga-tors," said the old sailor. "Those are beasts worth seeing! They'd snap a man's leg off! The Indians stuck big poles into their mouths and tipped them over. You can shoot an alligator with an arrow through the underside."

Pedro and Martin listened with wide-open eyes. They tried to picture what the new land of Indians and alligators would be like.

In the evening on deck, there was laugh-ter and pleasant talk. There was singing and dancing. Also a little man, called a dwarf, was aboard. He sang and danced well.

"Catalina must dance with him!" said the people. "They are the same size."

At first it was hard for Catalina to dance as the deck rose and fell. But soon her black curls were flying in the breeze. Her eyes were as bright as stars. She whirled about on the deck. People clapped and called for more. Pedro watched his sister proudly.

In nine days, the ships reached the Canary Islands. It was good to see trees, flowers, and fresh fruit again. People were tired of eating dried meat and salt fish. They were weary of the hard sea biscuit that they had to eat instead of bread. They were glad to have fresh water and fruit.

When the ships left the Canary Islands, there was less singing and dancing. People grew quieter. The most dangerous part of the trip lay ahead. The men talked of storms.

One afternoon, Pedro and Martin lay on deck looking up at the sky. Suddenly they saw the sun go under a gray cloud. The two boys started to their feet. A sudden wind nearly blew them off the deck. They caught hold of a rope and held tightly to it.

The masts of the ship began to rock back and forth across the dark sky. Sailors hurried to climb the masts to take in the sails, for such a wind would soon tear the sails to pieces. Pedro and Martin held their breath as the men climbed the ropes and tugged at the sails. The wind made the sails boom like thunder.

The next minute the rain began. The boys ran to the cabin door and hurried inside. They found everyone busy there. As the ship tossed, boxes and chests began to slide about the floor. They crashed into each other. "A child could be killed by one of them! " cried a woman. People were tying things with strong ropes. The boys rushed to help.

As night came on, the storm grew worse.

"Why did we ever leave Spain?" moaned a woman. "We shall all go to the bottom of the sea and be drowned."

As the ship rocked and tossed, the lanterns hanging in the cabin danced about like crazy things.

Some women wept. Others prayed.

Catalina's mother held her in her arms.

"All will be well, if God wills it," she said softly. "We have a strong ship and a brave captain."

It was well they had so fine a man for captain! He was standing and watching each wave, as it rose like a mountain of water before the ship. He ordered the ship steered a little to the left or to the right, so that it might rise safely over each huge wave.

The ship groaned and creaked like a rusty hinge. Suddenly water began pouring into the ship.

"Send men to the pumps!" the captain ordered.

There was a leak! Men had to pump the water out, or the ship would sink. The men worked as hard as they could. Pedro's father was in charge of the pumps. Pedro and Martin begged to help.

"Stay in the cabin with your mothers!" ordered Pedro's father.

Suddenly there came a deep boom like a cannon. The mainmast had broken. The top of the great pole fell into the sea. The ship gave a roll.

"The ship is sinking!" a woman screamed.

But this time the ship righted itself. Catalina buried her head in her mother's arms. She prayed for the Lord Jesus Christ to calm the sea. ❏

Chapter 3
Pedro's Knife

Waves broke across the deck in a mass of green water and white foam. They pounded against the cabin door. Then a giant wave struck. There was a crashing sound. Suddenly the great door of the cabin swung wide open. The bolt on the heavy door was broken. Water poured in. Wind and rain swept through the cabin.

"Quick, Pedro, quick!" cried his mother. "Close that door."

Martin was near, and the two boys jumped to their feet. A roll of the ship sent them tumbling to the floor. Pedro's head hit a sharp corner of a chest. He saw stars. For a minute he lay there. Then cold seawater splashed over him and brought him to his senses.

The two boys crawled to the door. It was swinging wildly back and forth as the ship rocked. Together they pushed the door shut. They tried to hold it shut, but the wind slammed it open again and knocked them down. Water washed about them. Up they jumped again and pushed the door.

"If only we could fasten it shut," panted Martin. "If only we had a strong nail to drive through the broken bolt."

Pedro thought of his knife. He reached to the case at his side. He pulled out his precious knife. He pushed it through the hole in the broken bolt.

"Give me something to pound it in with! " he cried. "Quick! Quick! We must drive it into the wood."

Martin pulled a small iron kettle loose from the rope that held it. The boys used the kettle to pound the knife through the bolt and into the wood. They drove the blade deep into the wood of the doorpost. Then they stood back against the wall, panting. The bolt held. The door stayed shut!

Pedro crept back to his mother. His head was bleeding. His mother wiped his face and tucked a blanket around him. He was glad to lie still.

All the long black night, the storm tossed the ship about. But, by morning, the rain stopped. The wind was not quite so fierce. People looked at one another. They dared to hope that they were safe.

A sailor who had come up from below pulled at the heavy cabin door to open it. He could not get Pedro's knife loose, so he broke it in half with a hammer. Pedro looked at it sadly.

Then Pedro and Martin crept out on deck. The fresh air smelled good. The boys looked out over the rough sea.

"Where are the other ships?" cried Pedro. There was not one in sight.

For many days the seas were rough. People were sick and miserable. The sea biscuit was wet. The dried meat and salt fish began to spoil. The drinking water was so stale that Catalina could hardly swallow it.

But at last land was sighted! At last the ship sailed into harbor. People hurried out on deck. The ship had reached the island of Puerto Rico. People from Spain had already built a town there.

"It is good to see houses and trees and dry earth again!" cried Catalina's mother.

Some of the ships were already in the harbor. People shouted to each other. They waved and called eagerly to friends.

But where were the other ships? Were they wrecked in the storm? Did they turn back to Spain? No one could say. Many a ship was lost in those days and never seen again.

The ships' carpenters worked hard before the ships set out again. There were many repairs to be made after the storm.

But at last the ships were ready to sail away. Florida lay ahead!

Time passed quickly. The sun shone. The women opened the chests and dried out the clothes that had been wet with salt water.

"My best red dress!" sighed one woman. "I can never wear it again."

But the ship was safe. Florida was near. People were eager and excited. Suddenly, one night, a comet flashed across the sky.

The people took this as a sign of God's favor.

It was two months since the ships had left Spain. At last, Florida came in sight. Pedro and Martin saw the low sandy shore. They looked for Indians and alligators, but all they saw were palms and palmettos, live oak and pine trees.

The general in charge of all these ships was named Menendez. In time, he chose the place to land.

The cannon on the ships roared. Drums beat and trumpets sounded as Menendez stepped ashore. He wore a shining suit of armor and a velvet cape. He carried the great gold and red flag of Spain.

The boys watched as General Menendez knelt and claimed the land for Spain.

"Look!" whispered Pedro suddenly to Martin. "Indians!"

A group of red warriors had slipped quietly from the deep woods to watch the strange new white men who had landed on their shores.

Later, as Pedro left the cabin of the ship, he looked sadly at his knife. The bolt on the door had been mended, but part of the knife was left sticking into the wood. The handle had been broken off. The blade was bent. Pedro put his hand on it. The precious knife! How he wished he had it back!

Just then Pedro heard a sound behind him. It was his father. He laid his hand on Pedro's arm.

"You did well, son," he said. "Your mother told me of the night of the storm. She told me how you and Martin fought to keep the door shut. If the cabin had flooded with water, the ship might have sunk. You did well. Here is another knife to take ashore

with you. It is a finer one."

He drew out his own knife and slipped it into Pedro's empty case. Pedro cried out his thanks. Then he followed his father out on deck. He was ready to land on this strange shore.

So, the people from Spain came to Florida in the year 1565. They started a town, which they called St. Augustine because land was sighted on that saint's day. They also built a fort.

Today, St. Augustine is a busy American city by the ocean. Each year, many people from all parts of the country go to visit this very old place.

It is the oldest city on the mainland of the United States. ❏

How People Lived on Sailing Ships

1. The first Spanish people who came to this country had far bigger boats than the Indians. This is how a ship looked.

2. Sailing ships usually had three masts. The tallest mast was the mainmast. The straightest trees were saved for masts.

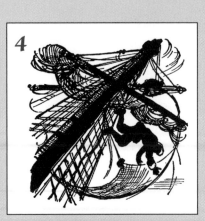

3. The ships had big canvas sails. The bars that held them were called yards. Sailors climbed along the yards to take in sails.

4. It was hard and dangerous work to take in the sails in a storm. Sometimes sailors fell overboard.

5. Sometimes in a storm a ship began to leak. Then men had to pump out the water. If the ship filled with water, it would sink. Men pumped night and day.

6. On pleasant days a sailing ship was a fine place to be. A fresh breeze blew. The ship flew over the waves. The sailors sat on deck and fished.

7. Food was cooked on deck in a big iron kettle. A fire was made in a box of sand. Enough wood for the whole trip had been brought along.

8. The inside of the ship looked like this. There were hard wooden bunks in the cabin. Food and water were stored in the hold below the cabins.

Questions

1. What is a pioneer?

2. Have you ever had experiences with boats? If so, what were they?

3. How was the ship that Pedro and Catalina came in different from our big ocean liners today?

4. Who were the key people in this story? Tell something about each one.

5. What is a comet?

6. Read Luke 8:22–25 and explain why it is proper to pray to Jesus during a storm.

Things to Do

1. Draw a picture of a ship like the one that brought Pedro and Catalina to America.

2. Collect pictures of all kinds of ships. Put up an exhibit on the bulletin board. Have an exhibit of ship models and toy boats.

3. These sentences tell what happened in the story. They are not in the right order. Which sentence tells what happened first? Which tells what happened next? Read the sentences in the right order.

   a. *Pedro and Catalina reached Florida at last.*
   b. *The cabin door blew open and water poured in.*
   c. *Pedro and Catalina sailed away from Spain.*
   d. *Pedro and Martin pounded the knife into the doorpost to hold the broken bolt.*

4. Bring an egg timer to school if you have one at home. See how long it takes for the sand to run through. Is the egg timer anything like an hour glass?

5. Which of the sentences below make you think of a storm at sea?

   a. *The waves were like mountains.*
   b. *The sails boomed like thunder.*
   c. *The Indians hunted alligators.*
   d. *The ship groaned and creaked like a mad thing.*
   e. *People sat on deck in the sun and fished.*

6. St. Augustine is the oldest city on the mainland of our country. The very oldest city in our country is on the island of Puerto Rico. See if you can find these places on the map.

   Spain   Florida   Puerto Rico

English Pioneers

A STORY OF PIONEERS IN VIRGINIA

In the year 1607, three small ships brought pioneers from England. They sailed up the James River, and they started a little town called Jamestown. It was named for King James of England.

It was hard work building homes in this new land. Many men had come to Jamestown hoping to find gold. They hoped to grow rich. Instead, they found hard work.

Many men grumbled. Many were hungry and sick. Then one man took charge. He was called Captain John Smith. He said that anyone who did not work should not eat. After that more work was done.

Trees were chopped down. A few poor huts were made. A fort was built. A wall was built around the little town. It was needed, for many of the Indians did not want the white men to come to this land.

Captain John Smith went often to the Indian villages. He bought corn from the Indians to keep the white men from starving. The English people had never seen Indian corn before. They learned to use the Indian corn for corn bread. They learned to plant it in the little fields outside the wall of the town. Corn became their most important food.

Captain John Smith did all that he could to keep peace with the Indians. But other Englishmen were not so wise as he. Often there was trouble with the Indians. People felt safer to have a fort with guns on it. People felt safer to have a wall around the town with a giant gate to shut at night.

At first there were only men in Jamestown. But soon mothers and children came across the water from England. It was hard for the mothers to make their families comfortable in this new, strange land. There were no stores to buy what was needed. A few things were brought from England. The people must make the rest for themselves.

What was it like living in Jamestown in those early days? The next story, "The Runaway," will tell you.

The Runaway

Chapter 4
Sally and Richard

Eight-year-old Sally sat in the doorway knitting. Knit, knit, knit! Was there ever an end to it?

Sally had to knit stockings for two brothers. Her fingers were never still. She must work all summer to be ready for winter.

In winter, feet were often cold and wet. There were no rubber boots in those days. There were no hard, dry sidewalks. In Jamestown there were only dirt paths, and they were often muddy. Warm knitted stockings were a comfort to cold feet in wet shoes.

Knit, knit, knit! Sally's fingers flew.

"Sally!" called her mother. "Watch the kettle that is hanging over the fire. Do not let the dinner burn. And mind the baby. I am taking the clothes to the river to wash."

It was easier to carry the wash to the river than to pull bucket after bucket of water from the well. Goodwife picked up a big bundle. The mother of a family was called "Goodwife" in those days, and a good wife she needed to be with all the work there was to do. Goodwife took a gourd filled with soft soap from the shelf.

Sally had helped her mother make that soap. It had been hard, hot work. They had saved grease and fats. Also, wood ashes had been saved from the fireplace. The ashes were put in a barrel and water was poured through them. That made the lye. When the lye was ready, the fat was boiled in a big soap kettle. Then the lye was put into it. "Lye was magic," Sally thought. Lye turned fat into clean soap.

Off to the river went Goodwife with her bundle of clothes on her head and her gourd of homemade soap in her hand. She was a good housekeeper. There was no better one in all Jamestown. Her linen was always white and clean. Her fire always burned in the fireplace.

That fire! Two years it had been burning. Never once had it gone out, day or night. Each evening, Goodwife covered the red coals with ashes. Every morning, she blew on the red coals and fed them little bits of dry sticks till the fire blazed up. Never once had her fire gone out.

Sometimes neighbors were careless. Sometimes they let their fires go out at night. Then they came running to Goodwife. They borrowed red coals to light their fires, because there were no matches in Jamestown. In those days, no one had ever heard of matches.

Sally went to the fire now, and peeked into the big iron kettle that was hanging in the fireplace. The deer meat smelled good. She put more wood on the fire. Then back she went to her knitting.

Small Richard played on the floor with some shells. He was only three. No small boy today would wear the clothes Richard wore. He had on a long skirt. Boys in those days did not wear pants until they were six or seven years old.

As Richard stood up, he stepped on his skirt. There was a loud tearing sound.

"Oh, dear," sighed Sally. "Another patch! There is more patch than dress now!"

It was hard to get cloth in this new land. Eight-year-old Sally knew how to mend and patch as well as knit.

Richard was pointing to a box on a shelf.

"No, no, Richard! You cannot have it," said Sally firmly.

Sally longed to peek into the box herself. Brother Ralph had brought home a baby squirrel. He had caught the tiny thing in the forest. He was taming it.

Ralph had made the box from pieces of wood. Sally had watched the squirrel curl up in it to sleep. The little animal had spread out its fluffy tail for a covering. Sally had laughed with delight.

Now Richard wanted to play with the squirrel. It was good that the shelf was high. Sally gave Richard a bit of cold corn bread. For a while he forgot the box. He ate the bread eagerly. He was hungry.

"The boys always seem to be hungry," sighed Sally. She was often hungry herself. Sometimes she sat and thought about good things to eat.

There was not much food in the house. Last year's corn was nearly gone. This year's corn was not yet ripe. In the morning, the children ate their hot corn meal and scraped the wooden bowls clean. They did not ask for more. They knew better.

But the men had shot a deer yesterday. There would be deer meat for dinner even though there was not much else. It smelled good as it cooked over the fire.

Richard grew sleepy. Sally put him in the old wooden cradle. Father had made that cradle. She rocked and sang as she knitted. Soon Richard's eyes closed.

Then Sally heard her mother calling. Goodwife wanted her to help in spreading the linen on the ground to whiten it in the sun. Oh, there were so many napkins to spread out! They needed a lot of them be-

cause there were no forks in Jamestown. People did not use forks in those days. There were only spoons and knives, and people ate their meat with their fingers.

"Sally!" called her mother. "Come and help me."

Sally ran out into the sunlight. Since so much white linen lay on the ground, it looked as though it had been snowing.

Goodwife was famous for her linen. She had spun the thread and woven it. She had brought a big chest of it with her from England. There might not be much to eat on her rough wooden table, but there were always fresh napkins.

While Sally worked, something was happening inside the house. ❏

Chapter 5
Outside the Gate

While Sally was away, something happened. A fly tickled Richard's face. In those days, there were no screens to keep flies out. Richard woke up. There was no one there. He sat up and looked around the cabin.

He saw the box on the shelf. The squirrel was inside. Richard rubbed his eyes. Then he climbed out of the cradle.

There was the big chest against the wall. Richard climbed onto it. He stood on his tiptoes. He could just reach the shelf. Little by little he pushed the box toward the edge.

The box fell. There was a crash! The top flew off. Out jumped the tiny animal. It ran around the room. Richard nearly fell off the chest as he tried to catch it.

The squirrel sat up and scolded him. Then it ran out the open door into the sunshine. Richard hurried after it.

When Sally came back, she found the room empty. She saw the box on the floor. There was no Richard asleep in the cradle. There was no sign of Richard in the small house.

Sally ran outdoors looking and calling. She ran to the neighbors, but no one had seen the runaway. Her mother had gone back to the river. She was out of sight.

Then Sally saw marks of small bare feet in the path. The marks led toward the gate in the wall that protected the town. Sally ran toward it. There was no guard at the gate. The men were all working in the fields outside the wall. No one had seen the runaway.

Sally's heart beat fast. Where was Richard? What had happened to him? Sally stopped at the gate. Beyond the fields was the forest. In the forest the trees were tall and dark. The forest was full of flowers and birds and sweet wild strawberries. But there were Indians and wild animals, too! The men always carried guns when they went into the woods.

For a moment, Sally stopped and prayed to God for help. Then she saw the marks of Richard's small bare feet. She followed them out the gate as fast as she could go. They led across a small cornfield. Then they went into the forest.

On and on Sally ran, following the tracks. Bushes caught her dress and tore it. There were ugly red scratches on her arms and legs. Then a vine tripped her up.

"Richard! Richard!" she called. "Where are you, Richard?"

Just then she heard an answer. There was a clearing in the woods ahead. She peered around the big trunk of a tree.

There was that little rascal! There was Richard! He was sitting on a grassy spot eating wild strawberries. His face and hands were red.

Sally threw herself down on the grass beside him and thanked the Lord for His help. She was hot and tired. Then she saw the berries. They looked like little glowing red coals. She,

too, began to eat. They were sweet and juicy.

Suddenly Sally remembered that they were far from home and alone.

"We must get home, Richard," she cried.

She pulled Richard to his feet. They started back. But which way should they go? For a minute Sally's heart stood still. Then she heard noises. Guns were being fired. There were shouts and cries.

It was easy now to tell which way to go. Sally started toward the sound of the guns. She dragged Richard after her. He was tired and scratched and crying.

Another gun was fired. What was happening?

"Hurry, Richard! Hurry!" cried Sally. "Something has happened!"

Perhaps Indians were attacking the fort. She must get Richard inside the wall. Perhaps the gate would be closed when they reached it. No one knew that they were outside. Sally half carried tired little Richard.

At last, she saw the gate ahead. It was still open. Sally ran through it and pulled Richard after her. Then she stopped for a minute to get her breath.

People were running through the little town with buckets in their hands. The men had rushed back from the fields at the sound of the guns. Now they were carrying buckets of water from the river.

Sally saw that smoke was pouring from the door of her home. ❏

Chapter 6
Friends in Need

There were no fire engines in those days. There were no fire hoses and pumps. The men stood in a line from the river to the house. They passed buckets of water from one man to the next as fast as they could.

Sparks had flown out from the fireplace in Sally's house. One spark had landed in Richard's cradle. The soft wool blanket had blazed up. Soon the wooden cradle was in flames. Then the wall started to burn. Wooden houses burned easily! By God's providence, a neighbor had seen the smoke. She had run for help. Ralph had fired a gun to call his father and the men from the fields.

Water was dashed on the flames. Bucketful after bucketful was thrown on the fire. At last, there was only smoke.

Sally followed her father into the kitchen. Tears ran down her face from the smoke and the smell of burning wool. But the fire was out. The house was saved.

Then everyone began to talk at once. It was sad that the blanket was burned. Also, it was too bad that the cradle was gone. The wall would have to be patched a little, but that was all the harm done. Everyone agreed that the house had been saved by God's grace!

"It was my fault! It was all my fault!" cried Goodwife when she heard Sally's story. "I never should have called Sally to help me. I should not have called her away. This would never have happened if I had not called her away."

She praised God and held Sally and Richard close in her arms. But just then, Sally looked toward the kettle.

"What will we eat for dinner?" she cried.

The deer meat was burned to cinders. There was nothing in the kettle but black coals. What were they going to eat? What were they going to do?

There were no freezers to go to in those days. There were no cans to open. There were no stores to run to. Thankfully, there were good neighbors. They did not have much for themselves, but they shared what they had.

With a little of this and a little of that, these good friends put a meal on the bare wooden table. As it so often is, those who have the least, share the most. They know what it is like to have children go to bed hungry.

At last, the family sat down to dinner. Father sat at the head of the table in the big chair that had come from England. The rest of the family sat on

three-legged wooden stools that Father had made from logs.

Before they ate, Father bowed his head in prayer. He gave a prayer of thanksgiving to God for all His goodness and mercy.

"Oh," thought Sally, "there is so much for which to be thankful! God is good, indeed."

She was thankful that Richard was safe. She was thankful that the house had not burned to the ground. She was thankful that the neighbors had given them something to eat, because she was very hungry.

Suddenly there was a little sound at the window. Everyone looked that way. A tiny nose peeked in. Two very bright eyes looked at them.

"It's the baby squirrel!" cried Sally. "It has come back!"

The tiny thing ran to Ralph. It cuddled down inside his jacket. It was lonely. The baby squirrel had missed him.

"That's something else for which to be thankful," said Sally.

That evening the family sat around the open fire as usual. Goodwife was busy mending. Sally knitted as fast as she could. Ralph worked with his knife, cutting out a wooden mixing bowl from a piece of oak wood. He was making it for his mother. And Richard sat on his father's lap.

As they worked in the evening, their father often told stories of the old days.

Sometimes he told of the trip across the ocean from England. Sometimes he told of the first hard winters in Jamestown.

This evening, Sally asked for the story that she liked best. It was about the little Indian princess, Pocahontas, who had saved the life of Captain John Smith.

Pocahontas had been brought up in the forest. She was the daughter of a great Indian chief named Powhatan. On one occasion, Powhatan's brother captured Captain John Smith and brought him to the great chief. Powhatan ordered one of his warriors to kill the white man, but Pocahontas threw herself between the warrior and the white man. She begged her father to save the man's life. Her father looked at her in surprise. Then he gave the sign, and the warrior stepped back. Captain John Smith was saved.

Sally had often seen Pocahontas in Jamestown. Pocahontas was a graceful, slender Indian girl. Many times the little princess had helped the English settlers. She had brought them corn when they were starving. She also had warned them of Indian attacks. After several years, she became a Christian and was baptized

with the name Rebecca.

Of all the stories that her father told, Sally liked best the story of Pocahontas.

At last, Sally's head began to nod. Richard was sound asleep in his father's arms. Since his cradle was burned, he would sleep with Sally in her bed in the corner of the kitchen.

Sally felt herself lifted up in her father's strong arms. She was carried across the room. Her mother slipped off Sally's clothes. Soon she and Richard were tucked safely in the little bed.

Ralph climbed to the loft where he slept. He carried his squirrel with him. Goodwife covered her red coals carefully so that the fire would keep for the night. Soon all was dark and quiet in the little house in Jamestown. ❑

How Soap Was Made

1. Soap making was hard, hot work! Everyone dreaded the day. Scraps of fat and grease from cooking were saved in a big iron kettle.

2. All winter, wood ashes were saved in a barrel. Water was poured in. It soaked slowly through the ashes and made lye.

3. The lye had to be strong to make good soap. When an egg would float in the lye, it was strong enough. Only a little of the egg should show.

4. A fire was built under the big kettle outdoors. The boys chopped the wood. Smoke got in everyone's eyes. Everyone hated the smell of hot fat.

5. The lye was poured carefully into the hot fat. Lye burns. It must not splash on hands or clothes. Be careful!

6. The lye was stirred with a long wooden spoon. If it was just the right strength, it turned the grease into soap.

7. The top of the soap was hard enough to cut into cakes. The rest was put into a soft-soap barrel. It was dipped out with a gourd.

8. At the end of the day, everyone was tired out. But there was soap enough on hand to last a long time. They were careful not to waste it.

Questions

1. What are some things, which the pioneers made at home, that we buy in stores today?

2. Why did the people at Jamestown build a wall around their town?

3. From where did the people who settled Jamestown come?

4. From where did the people who settled St. Augustine come?

5. What did you eat for breakfast? What did you have that the first settlers in Jamestown could not have? Why can we have more things today?

6. Explain how Sally helped her mother make soap.

Things to Do

1. If you can, bring a gourd or an ear of corn to class. How did the pioneers use gourds? Learn the names of the different parts of the corn:

   husk   *stalk*   *silk*   *ear*   *kernel*

2. Plant a few kernels of corn in a pot of soil. Place the pot in the sunshine, and keep the soil moist. What happens? Pound some kernels between stones to make corn meal.

3. Before the days of matches, a fire was hard to start. If you know a Boy Scout, get him to show you one way to start a fire without matches. **Do not try to start a fire without your parents permission!**

4. If someone in your family can knit, ask them to bring their knitting to class. What can you see in the room that is knitted?

5. Act out something that happened in this story. Let one or both of your parents guess which scene it is.

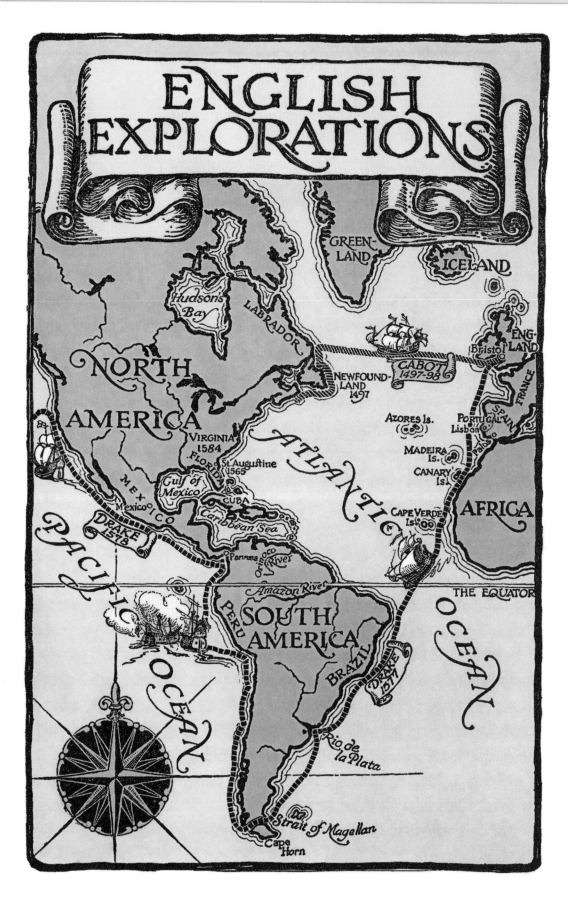

Pilgrim Pioneers from England

A STORY OF PIONEERS IN PLYMOUTH

Other pioneers, called Pilgrims, came from England. They did not come to find gold. Instead, they came to find a place where they could live and worship God in peace. They just wanted to have their own godly church. In England, the Pilgrims could not live as they believed the Bible required.

In 1620, the Pilgrims came to this country in a ship named the *Mayflower*. It was a small ship, but it carried over a hundred people. As the *Mayflower* made its way over the ocean, a new baby boy was born named Oceanus Hopkins.

The Pilgrims landed at Plymouth. It was near Christmas day when the Pilgrims came ashore, but there was no giving of Christmas presents. The Pilgrims were a joyful people, who were serious about serving God. They did not believe in making merry when there was work to do.

The men started to cut down trees, but they were not Christmas trees. One big house for all to share must be built, and built quickly. All who could work must help, for the cold weather was upon them.

The Pilgrims did not build log cabins. It would have been better if they had. Log cabins were easier to make than board houses. They were warmer. But the Pilgrims did not know how to make log cabins. They split and sawed logs into beams and boards. They fastened the beams together with wooden pegs. They had brought a few nails with them, but nails were hard to get. Each nail had to be made by hand.

What was it like, building the first house in Plymouth? There were no cement mixers or steel beams. There were no brickyards to bake clay into red bricks. There were no lumberyards where the Pilgrims could buy smooth, sweet-smelling boards. There were no stores where one could get nails and locks. There were no doors or window frames or window glass to be had.

But there were tall trees. There were men with strong hands and arms. They had brought axes and saws from England. They had also brought sharp iron wedges to split logs into planks.

What was it like, building the first house in Plymouth? The next story will tell you.

House Raising

Chapter 7
In the Forest

"Do you think we will see Indians?" asked Thomas. "The less we see of Indians the better!" said a man. "The other day, an arrow missed my hat by an inch!"

Thomas followed his father and several other men toward the forest. It was a cold, damp day. The tall trees were black against the gray winter sky.

The boy looked back at the *Mayflower*. The ship looked small and lonely as it lay in the harbor. He was tired of being shut up in that ship! He was glad to be ashore at last. The men had been ashore before, searching and hunting for a good place to build homes. The women and children had been left on board.

There were only a few trees near the shore where they landed. Back from the shore was a wooded hill. Thomas followed the men to the woods. He peered between the great trunks of the trees. He was excited, and still he was afraid. What was in those woods?

Something moved beside him. Thomas gave a cry. The men came running with their guns.

"What is it?" they shouted. "What do you see? Indians?"

A slow porcupine walked heavily across the dead leaves. The men began to laugh.

But one man said in anger, "Keep your cries to yourself, lad! You've no business to frighten us. Use your head, or stay with the women on board the ship!"

Thomas turned red. He had not meant to cry out. The men soon forgot him. They chose strong oak trees to cut. Thirty or forty trees would be needed for the house. Soon the woods were filled with the sounds of chopping.

Those woods had never heard such sounds before! Frightened deer ran swiftly away. A bear turned over in his winter bed. Was a storm blowing the trees down? Squirrels scolded the strangers for spoiling their winter homes.

"Count my strokes, lad," said Thomas's father. "They say ten strokes of an ax should bring down a fair-sized tree."

Chips flew. The smell of fresh-cut wood filled the air. But ten strokes did not bring down the tree. Thomas counted ten and then ten more.

His father stopped to rest. His hands were sore.

"Let me try," begged Thomas.

He was eager to help. He gripped the ax as he had seen his father do. Thomas tried to give the tree a heavy blow. Instead, he hardly hit the tree. He dropped the ax. Then he tipped himself over and fell to the ground.

"The boy's not big enough for an ax," said one of the men. "He will cut his foot open the next thing you know. He should be back with the women and children."

Thomas bit his lip. He wanted to help. But everything he did was wrong.

"Look out!" someone shouted. "The first tree is coming down!"

A tall proud tree began to tip. There was a crashing of branches. The tree fell faster and faster until it struck the ground. Then the tree lay still.

It was a great sight to see that big tree lying low. It had been so tall and beautiful. Now it lay so helpless. The men walked along the broad trunk and cut off the branches. Here was a place a boy could help.

"Take this hatchet and cut the smaller branches into firewood," called his father. "But watch out, son. Do not cut yourself. Think about what you are doing. Use your head."

Thomas worked away. The wind was cold and damp, but he was soon warm from the work. He piled his wood, ready to carry to the ship.

The men sawed the trunk of the tree to the right length for a great beam. Then they cut the sides square with their axes. At last the first beam for the new house was ready. Many more would be needed.

Down came another tree. The woods were filled with the crashing sound. Tree after tree fell. The short winter day was soon over. Evening was coming on.

The woods grew dim and dark. The men were weary and hungry. It was time to stop work.

Two men tied a rope to one of the beams and dragged it down to the shore. Thomas wanted to help. He only seemed to get in the way.

"Wherever I step I fall over that boy!" cried one man. "He is everywhere and always in the way!"

Thomas stood back with a sigh.

"Go get your firewood," said his father softly. "Carry as big a load as you can, and keep out of the men's way. Use your head, son."

Some of the men spent the night in small bark huts that they had built. Thomas and his father went back to the ship. It was warm in the little cabin of the *Mayflower*. His mother had hot food ready. When they had eaten, Thomas leaned over the tiny new baby. He stretched out his hand, which was red from the cold, and the baby gripped his finger.

"I never saw such little hands," said Thomas.

His father looked at the baby. His face was serious and concerned.

"We must get a house built to keep the little ones warm and safe," he said. "There is no time to spare." ❏

Chapter 8
Logs into Beams

The ends of the beams were cut so that they would fit together. Holes were bored in them. Pegs were needed to hold the beams together.

The next day, all the boys from the ship were set to work cutting pegs. A big fire blazed on the shore. The boys worked near it.

At first, Thomas worked as fast as he could. But soon he grew tired. Smoke from the fire blew in his eyes. It seemed to him as though he had cut enough pegs to hold the world together!

Suddenly the sharp knife slipped and cut his hand. Thomas gave a cry as blood came from his finger.

"He is afraid of a little blood," laughed one boy foolishly. Thomas frowned. He walked to the brook nearby. He broke a hole in the ice. The cold water would stop the bleeding. Why did he cry out so easily? Why did he do everything wrong?

Just then Thomas forgot his troubles. His finger had stopped bleeding. He cut a strong willow branch that grew by the water. He bent it against his foot. What a fine bow it would make! He would make a bow to shoot as the Indians did!

Thomas bent the branch. Then he strung a piece of string across it. Now for an arrow! He chose a forked stick and sharpened the point.

"See what I have," he called, as he went back to the fire.

The boys crowded around him.

"Let's see you shoot," they said.

"Stand back!" Thomas answered.

He fitted the arrow to the bow. He pulled the string. The arrow sped through the air. It went faster and farther than Thomas had expected.

A man had just finished making a window for the new house. He had no glass, and so he had stretched heavy paper across the opening. The paper was oiled and would let in the light.

Thomas sent his arrow straight through the paper!

"See what you have done, you rascal!" shouted the man. "Have you no head to use? It's a pity your father did not drop you overboard!"

"I meant no harm, Sir," said Thomas. "I will do whatever I can to make up."

The man gave a grunt. The boy had nerve at any rate.

"I'm splitting a log into planks to make the front door," he said. "Hold this wedge for me."

Slowly Thomas put out his hand to hold the wedge. He gripped the wedge tightly, and he tried to hold it still. The man raised his hammer. But it was hard for the boy to hold his hand still with the hammer so close to his fingers.

Up went the hammer ready for a blow. It was too much for Thomas! Before he knew what he was doing, he jumped back. He dropped the wedge.

"Here's a pretty mess!" cried the man. "You can shoot an arrow through a window and spoil a day's work. But you are afraid to hold a wedge! Get away with you.

You are more trouble than you are help!"

Sadly, Thomas went back to cutting pegs. Would he ever learn to use his head?

Ellen joined him by the fire. She was just his age.

He always watched out for Ellen. She had no father or mother. She had come to help one of the women on the *Mayflower*. She seemed small and alone. She held her long cape close around her, but

she looked cold and white.

The boys began to laugh at Thomas. Suddenly Ellen's eyes grew big and dark. She turned on the boys and she stamped her foot.

"He is better than any of you!" she cried. "You wait and see! You laugh and you make fun, but there is not one of you as quick and as kind as Thomas."

Ellen turned and ran back to the women. They were heating water in a big iron kettle over an open fire for their washing. ❑

Chapter 9
The House Raising

At last, the frame for the new house was ready to be raised.

Everyone gathered to help or to watch. At least everyone came who was well enough to be up. Many of the people lay ill and weak because of the long trip, poor food, and cold winter weather.

Thomas stood by Ellen. He was eager and excited as he watched the men working. How much he wanted to help!

But his father said softly, "Keep out of the way, son. You are too young for this heavy work."

One side of the frame was ready to be lifted into place. The men had long forked poles. They used them to lift the side into place. They struggled and strained as they raised the heavy load.

A man climbed carefully up the frame. Then the next side was raised. The man tried to reach it so that he could fasten the two sides together.

But the second side would not go where it should.

"Push it a little nearer!" shouted the men below. "No, easy there! That's too far!"

It seemed as though the frame were teasing them. It seemed as though it did not want to go into place.

If only the man had an extra hand. He must hold on with one hand while he reached for the second side with the other. He leaned over as far as he dared.

"Hold it! Hold it!" cried the men below.

The heavy frame began to tip! If it fell, there would be much hard work lost. People gasped with horror. The men struggled to hold up the frame. They needed the house so badly. They had worked so hard!

Then Thomas sprang forward. He could see clearly just what should be done. He knew he could jerk that frame into place. Before he thought about what he was doing, he cried out, "I can fix it!"

"You!" cried a rude man. "You will only make trouble!"

But Thomas had darted forward. He started up the frame like a cat. He was light and small. A second man could not go up the frame without tipping it. Perhaps a boy could.

People held their breath as they watched him. Some called to him to come back. Some shouted to him to go on. As he reached the top of the frame, Thomas felt dizzy. He did not like high places. He stopped for a minute. Then he saw Ellen below. She was waving her hand and calling to him, "Go on! Go on, Thomas!" On he went.

In another minute, he had pulled the frame into place. The holes fitted neatly, one right over the other.

In went the pegs to hold the two sides together. The frame stood strong and firm.

Thomas crept back. His hands were full of splinters. His clothes were torn. But he was happy. He was happier than he had ever been.

"The boy was as quick as a cat!" people said. "He has saved the house! He used his head this time! He is one to watch!"

Thomas slipped to Ellen's side. She smiled at him proudly. He stood beside her as they watched the last beams raised and hammered into place.

"You have torn your jacket," whispered Ellen. "But I will mend it for you."

When the frame of the house was up, planks were fastened to the beams to make the sides. Logs split in half made the floor. The roof was thatched with bundles of coarse reeds tied with grapevines.

A big fireplace was built of stone. The chimney was made of small logs covered with clay to keep them from burning. A strong pole of green wood was put across the chimney to hold the kettles.

It was an exciting day when the first fire was lit in the new house. Women hurried here and there unpacking chests and cooking food. The boys ran back and forth carrying loads from the shore into the house. Then big iron kettles were hung over the fire. Soon the good smell of food filled the room. The house was done!

There were only one house and a few bark huts, but the people could live together this first winter. They had been together in the cabin of the *Mayflower*. They

were used to living together.

Later each family would have its own house.

And so the town of Plymouth was started.

The first year was very hard for the Pilgrims, just as it had been hard for the people in Jamestown. Many died. But the well people cared tenderly for those who were ill. They worked hard. They prayed to God for His help and sought to glorify the Lord Jesus Christ.

Then one day, an Indian walked into town. Children ran in fear and hid behind their mothers. Men reached for their guns. But the Indian raised his hand as a sign of peace. He came as a friend.

Later he came again with another Indian, who had been to England and spoke some English. The Indians helped the Pilgrims to plant corn. They showed them how to put a small fish in each corn hill so that the plant would grow well. They gave them seeds of beans and squash.

In the fall, when the corn and beans and squash were ripe, there was happiness in Plymouth. There would be food, not much, but some, for the winter. A day was set aside for thanksgiving.

A great Indian chief and ninety Indians came to the little town for that thanksgiving feast. They brought wild turkeys and five deer.

It was our first Thanksgiving Day. It was a day of feasting. It was also a day of prayer to Almighty God who is the Giver of all good things. ❑

How The Pilgrims Built Their Houses

1. First, men chose tall oak trees. Thirty or forty trees were needed for one house. The men chopped the trees down.

2. Boys helped chop off branches. Then the men cut the sides of the logs square for beams. They used their sharp axes.

3. Ends of beams were cut so that they would fit neatly together. Pegs were used instead of nails. Pegs were driven through holes to hold the beams in place.

4. Some of the logs were split into planks. The men pounded wedges into the logs. The wedges split the logs into planks. Saws were used to cut the planks.

5. When one side of the house had been put together, the men came to raise it. They pushed up the frame with poles.

6. Doors and windows were made. If there was no glass, oiled paper was used. A wooden latch held the door shut.

7. The roof was thatched with bundles of straw or reeds. The bundles were laid in rows and tied in place. The rows overlapped.

8. The fireplace was made of stone. The first chimneys were made of logs covered with clay. It was a happy day when the first fire was lit.

Questions

1. Where did the Pilgrim women and children stay while the first house was being built?
2. What did the Pilgrims use in place of nails as they built their homes?
3. What materials did the Pilgrims use when making their houses?
4. What things did young people do in Plymouth to help their parents?
5. Why did the Pilgrims celebrate Thanksgiving Day?
6. How did the Indians help the Pilgrims?

Things to Do

1. Make Indian headbands. Cut a strip of strong paper two inches wide. Cut out two feathers. Color them. Paste them on the band. Fasten the band with a clip.
2. If you have a bead-making kit, make an Indian bracelet with a diamond-shaped pattern. Visit your local library or craft store for more ideas, or search the Internet under "Indian bead kits."
3. Obtain dried corn from the store and grind it up to make old-fashioned corn bread.
4. Write a short poem of thanksgiving to God. Ask your parents to help you put together a special feast, complete with turkey, deer meat, and squash.
5. Ask your parents to help you make oiled paper so you can see the type of windows that the Pilgrims used.

Pioneers from Holland

A STORY OF DUTCH PIONEERS

Pioneers from Holland also came to the land of North America. People who live in Holland are called Dutch. The Dutch pioneers started their settlement where New York City stands today. They named it New Amsterdam after the Dutch city of Amsterdam.

As soon as they could, the people in New Amsterdam built Dutch houses like the ones in Holland. Soon they built a big Dutch windmill. Blue-eyed Dutch children played near the water.

Dutch mothers scrubbed the floors of their houses and tried to keep them as clean as the houses in old Amsterdam.

The Dutch pioneers had an easier time than the people in Jamestown and Plymouth. Dutch traders had been coming for some years to trade for furs with the Indians. They had built a few rough houses and started a fort. When the first fathers and mothers and children arrived, they found a fort and a few rough houses ready for them.

Then, one day, a ship sailed into the harbor with a very special load. The sea gulls flew about it, crying with surprise. Indians paddled out in their canoes to look in wonder.

The ship was loaded with cows and sheep and pigs. They were pioneers too!

It was a great day for New Amsterdam when that ship sailed into the harbor. There were several islands in the harbor. One large island was very close to the mainland. The ship stopped near it. There were no pastures ready for the animals on the mainland. The precious animals would be safer on the island at first.

What was it like on that day? How did the Dutch people feel? What did the Indians think? How had the Dutch sailors managed to bring cows so far?

The next story will tell you.

*Peter
and His
Cow Trinka*

Chapter 10
The Landing

Peter stood beside his cow Trinka. There was a smile on his face. There would have been a smile on Trinka's face if cows could smile. The trip from Holland to America was safely over.

"But really Trinka hardly knew she was not standing in her own barn," said Peter proudly. "She is a wonderful cow. She gives more cream than milk. She is gentle and kind. Her calves are just like her."

Peter's sister Juliana stood beside him. She was four years old. She agreed with all he said.

There were a few sheep and goats and pigs aboard, but the hold of the ship was filled with cows. No other cow could compare with Trinka!

Trinka had switched her tail and mooed gently all the way across the Atlantic Ocean. She had been well cared for each day. Big tanks to hold water had been built into the ship. Each day Peter had pumped up water for Trinka to drink and carried it to her in a pail. Clean white sand covered the water tanks.

Each cow had her own stall. Each cow stood in her own stall on the pure white sand. There was plenty of sweet hay aboard for the cows to eat. An extra ship sailed nearby with extra water and extra hay.

Each cow had a man or boy to care for her. Two of the precious animals had died at sea. It was a sad thing! But the rest were well and fat.

Trinka had never looked more beautiful.

"One would think she were going to the Fair," sighed Peter.

Peter had brushed her coat until it shone. He had rubbed her horns and hoofs. Juliana had given him her best red ribbon. He had tied it on Trinka's tail.

Now Trinka was ready to land in this strange new country. Peter led her out on deck.

He could see the thatched roofs of the tiny town of New Amsterdam near the water's edge. Woods came close about it. Were there Indians in those woods? What would the Indians say to Trinka, and what would Trinka say to the Indians?

But the cows were not to land in New Amsterdam. There were no pastures ready near that town. The cows might wander into the woods and be killed by wolves or bears. Peter trembled at the thought. He would fight any bear or wolf that came near Trinka!

The cows were to be landed on a small island in the harbor. The island was a safer place for them than New Amsterdam until pastures were ready. The ship sailed close to the shore of the small island. Planks were laid from deck to land. There were loud mooings and shouting and much noise. Some of the animals did not wish to go ashore.

Juliana ran to her mother and stayed close to her. Peter watched anxiously while his father and the other men pushed and pulled the animals down the plank. At last, it was Trinka's turn.

"Trinka, little one," whispered Peter. "Come with me, Trinka. Do not be afraid!"

He led her gently toward the plank.

"Come, little one," urged Peter.

But Trinka would not come. She mooed and turned back. She had decided that she did not want to be a pioneer. She wanted to go back to Holland.

"Get off there!" shouted a man.

Never had Trinka been spoken to in so rough a way. She tossed her head wildly.

"Please, Trinka, take just one little step for me!" Peter begged.

Suddenly something happened that surprised both Peter and Trinka. A pig ran loose. Men tried to catch it, but it is easier to catch lightning than a pig. It ran squealing toward the plank.

Right between Trinka's legs ran the pig. Trinka gave a bellow of surprise. She ran down the plank as fast as she could go. Peter was in the way. There was no place for him to go except into the water. There was a great splash. Trinka and the pig reached land. Peter did not.

"Help! Help!" shouted the people. "Save the boy!"

They pulled Peter from the water.

"To think that Trinka would do this to me!" thought Peter as he stood with water running off him. "Before all the world you give me a dunking! Oh, Trinka! Think of the hay and water I have carried for you!"

His mother hurried Peter to the cabin for dry clothes. Juliana looked seriously at him with her big blue eyes. When he was dressed again, she followed him out on deck. Together they stood watching the animals galloping around the island. They could tell Trinka by the red ribbon on her tail.

At last the animals grew tired and settled down. Trinka lay down beneath a tree. She was glad to find that she had a little cud left. It was a wonder!

Slowly she began to chew. ❏

Chapter 11
New Amsterdam

A few days later, a ship loaded with horses arrived. Peter watched the men unload them. His father and mother and Juliana had gone ashore to stay with friends in New Amsterdam. Peter was still living on the ship. He wished to be near Trinka. Each day he went ashore to be with her.

The small island seemed alive with animals. Indians paddled out to look at the wonder. They had never dreamed there were such beasts. For the Indians had no horses or cows until the white men brought them across the ocean.

There were deer and buffaloes and wolves and bears in this new land. But those animals are not good ones to tame. You cannot ride a buffalo. You cannot milk a bear.

There was not enough grass on the small island for so many animals.

"We must take the horses and cows across to New Amsterdam, where there is more grass for them to eat," said the men. "It will be dangerous in the woods with no pastures or fences ready. The boys will have to stay with them and watch them carefully."

"How will the animals get over?" asked Peter.

"We will carry some of the animals over in small boats," said the men. "Some of the animals can swim."

"Trinka could never swim," cried Peter in horror. "I do not believe that Trinka knows how to swim!

"Get her into a boat, then," called the men.

They were pulling one cow in backward by her tail.

Peter talked gently to Trinka. He explained everything to her while she slowly chewed her cud.

She had lost her red ribbon. Peter thought that an Indian boy had taken it. He saw two Indian boys in a canoe near the island. One had a red ribbon round his head. The Dutch boy and the Indian boys looked at each other with interest.

The Indian boys looked at Peter's heavy wool suit and wooden shoes. Peter looked at the Indian boys. They wore only moccasins and strips of deerskin. As he looked, one Indian boy dived from the canoe into the water. He swam swiftly toward the mainland.

So now, as Peter led Trinka toward the boat, she had no ribbon on her tail. She had burrs in her coat, and her hoofs were muddy, but she was still a fine cow.

"Come into the boat with me, Trinka," said Peter softly.

But the little boat rocked up and down on the waves. Trinka did not like its looks.

"There, there, little one," murmured Peter.

Then an idea came to him. If Trinka could not see the boat, she would not be afraid.

He pulled off his coat. Under it he wore his best linen shirt. Peter took the shirt off carefully. He tied it about Trinka's head and over her eyes.

"Come, Trinka!" he said firmly.

But Trinka had other plans. She could see nothing. It had become dark. Clearly it was night. She would lie down and go to sleep.

The men in the boat began to laugh. It was too much for Peter. His patience was gone!

"Get up!" Peter said sharply to Trinka.

But Trinka only chewed her cud.

Peter grasped her tail and gave it a pull. Trinka started to get up, but then she settled back again. Peter did something that he had never expected to do. He gave Trinka a kick with his wooden shoe.

Trinka was so surprised that she scrambled to her four feet. Peter gave a tug at the rope. Down to the boat went Trinka. Peter gave a sigh of relief as she stood with her head on his shoulder. She slowly chewed her cud as the boat moved across the water.

Mother and Juliana were on shore waving to him as he landed. Peter quickly took his shirt off Trinka's head and put it on himself. It was wrinkled, but it was still as white as snow.

Proudly he led Trinka through the little town of New Amsterdam. Dutch children stopped playing to run along beside him and cheer. Dutch mothers stopped scrubbing their floors to run to their doors.

"As fine a cow as any in Holland!" they cried. "A wonderful cow! Now we shall have milk and thick yellow cream and butter and fat cheeses."

"This is a fine thing for the town," said the men as they smoked their long Dutch pipes.

"The rest of the cows will be over before night," called Peter happily. "And horses and sheep and pigs as well!" ❑

Chapter 12
"Come Quickly!"

Each morning, Peter and two other boys drove the cows to graze outside the town. Each morning Peter went through the narrow streets of the little town. He blew on a cow's horn. People ran to open their barn doors. Out came the cows to follow Trinka.

All day, Peter and the boys watched the cows carefully. It was pleasant at the edge of the woods. Often Indians came by with loads of beaver furs to sell in New Amsterdam. Often hunters came past.

At the end of the day, the boys drove the cows home. Each cow knew its own barn. Dutch women ran to their kitchen doors. The doors were cut in half. There were no screen doors in those days. The lower half of the door was shut to keep cows or pigs from coming into the kitchen by mistake. The top half of the door stood open for air and light.

Out ran the Dutch women as Peter came by with the cows. Each woman carried a milking pail to hold the milk from the cows.

One day, the cows wandered farther into the woods than usual. Peter was troubled. The boys ran after the cows and drove them back. When it was time to start home, something dreadful happened.

Some of the cows would not go. Some walked slowly as though in pain. Some mooed loudly.

Peter was worried. He ran on ahead for help.

"Come quickly!" he shouted to the first men he saw. "All is not well with the cows!"

The men dropped their work and came running.

"What has happened?" they shouted.

"What is the matter?" they called.

Peter could only point to the cows. Some were lying down. Some were groaning. Peter was thankful to see that Trinka was still on her feet.

"Drive the well cows home, Peter," called the men. "We will see what we can do for these poor beasts."

Peter hurried along the streets with the well cows. He drove those he had with him to their barns. People called to him from every side.

"Where are our cows?" some asked anxiously. "Why didn't you bring all the cows home?"

No one slept in New Amsterdam that night. Twenty of the cows were ill. Twenty of the precious cows that had come so far and been tended so carefully. It was a sad thing indeed!

"They must have eaten some strange weed," said the men. "It has poisoned them. There is little we can do."

In the barn, Peter sat beside Trinka. He sat and watched every breath she took. Not for a moment would he leave her. Had Trinka eaten the poison?

"Oh, my Trinka! Oh, my little Trinka!" whispered Peter.

Juliana brought him his supper, but he could hardly eat. She brought him fresh

fried cakes that his mother had just made for him. But Peter could not even touch them. He held a lantern in his hand and he looked Trinka over from head to tail.

She seemed calm and peaceful. She was chewing her cud. But perhaps the poison had not yet begun to work.

A neighbor brought sad news. Several of the cows had died. Peter gave a groan. He looked at Trinka.

"You had better go to your bed, Peter," said his father.

Peter was sad. He did not want to leave Trinka, so he asked his father if he could stay with his precious cow. His father said, "Son, you may stay here tonight."

"Please do not die, Trinka!" he whispered.

At last, Trinka lay down to sleep. Peter settled on the hay beside her. Once she had a bad dream and gave a loud groan. Peter jumped to his feet in fear.

But she only turned over and went to sleep again. In the morning, Juliana found Peter sound asleep, with his head on Trinka's back. But Trinka was safe. She was as strong and well as ever.

It was a sad procession that went to pasture the next day. Nineteen cows were dead. But the others were alive and safe. Trinka led the way down the street. Peter and the boys drove the precious animals to a different part of the woods.

The cows that did not die soon had calves. Before long the barns of New Amsterdam were filled with fine cattle. The housewives skimmed thick yellow cream from the pans of milk. They churned cream into butter. They made cheeses as big as your head.

It was a fine thing for New Amsterdam to have the cows.

But how did New Amsterdam become New York? One day, when Peter was much older, and Trinka was a grandmother, a strange thing happened.

English warships came sailing into the harbor.

The Dutch governor of New Amsterdam at that time was a godly leader named Peter Stuyvesant. Peter Stuyvesant had only one leg, so he wore a wooden one. He marched around the town with his wooden leg, and he ordered the men to fight the English.

But the English had more guns and cannon than the Dutch did. The Dutch men would not fight.

Peter Stuyvesant was a brave soldier. He stamped about the fort with his wooden leg. He ordered his men to fire, but they would not fight.

"It is foolish to shed blood for nothing," they said. "If we fight, our town will be destroyed. Our wives and children will be killed. We do not have enough guns or soldiers. There is no hope of winning!"

At last, Peter Stuyvesant had to surrender. He could not fight alone. Down came the Dutch flag from the fort. Up went the English flag.

The English ships had been sent by the brother of the king of England. He was called the Duke of York. So the name of New Amsterdam was changed to New York. And that is its name today!

But today the flag of New York City is still orange, white, and blue, like the old flag of Holland.

Each year New York City grows larger and larger. ❏

How Butter Was Made

1. First, the cows were milked. Buckets of milk were carried to the house.

2. The milk was poured into pans to set. Slowly the thick yellow cream rose to the top.

3. The next morning, the good housewife skimmed off the cream. Some of it she used on wild strawberries or puddings. The rest went into the churn.

4. When the churn was full of cream, it was time to begin the butter making. The dasher in the churn was worked up and down, up and down.

5. It was hard work. At last, little yellow lumps of butter began to show. Soon the butter was so thick that the dasher could hardly be moved.

6. Then the butter was skimmed out. Buttermilk was left in the churn. It was good to drink. Everyone liked fresh butter on bread, too.

7. The buttermilk was pressed out, and the butter was well washed in fresh water. It was patted into shape with paddles.

8. If the butter was to be kept for long, it was salted. Salted butter kept better. It was packed in little tubs.

Questions

1. What name is given to the people of Holland?

2. Why did the settlers want cows and horses?

3. Who was Peter Stuyvesant?

4. Find New York City on the map. Why is so large a place only a little dot on the map?

5. Why were the animals not taken to New Amsterdam first? Why are fences important?

6. Explain how New Amsterdam became New York.

Things to Do

1. These are some of the important names in this book. See if you can read them aloud.

St. Augustine	*New York*	*Plymouth*
Peter Stuyvesant	*Pilgrims*	*Florida*
Captain John Smith	*Jamestown*	*Holland*
New Amsterdam	*Pocahontas*	*Menendez*

2. Make a Dutch windmill out of sticks or draw a picture of one.

3. Which direction is north on your map? Which direction is north in your bedroom?

4. If you can, bring a compass to class. If someone, like your parents, can bring a magnet and a needle, you can make a compass. Rub the needle on the magnet. Float the needle on a tiny bit of paper in a cup of water. The needle will swing toward north. Ask your teacher to explain how a compass would help a sailor or hiker.

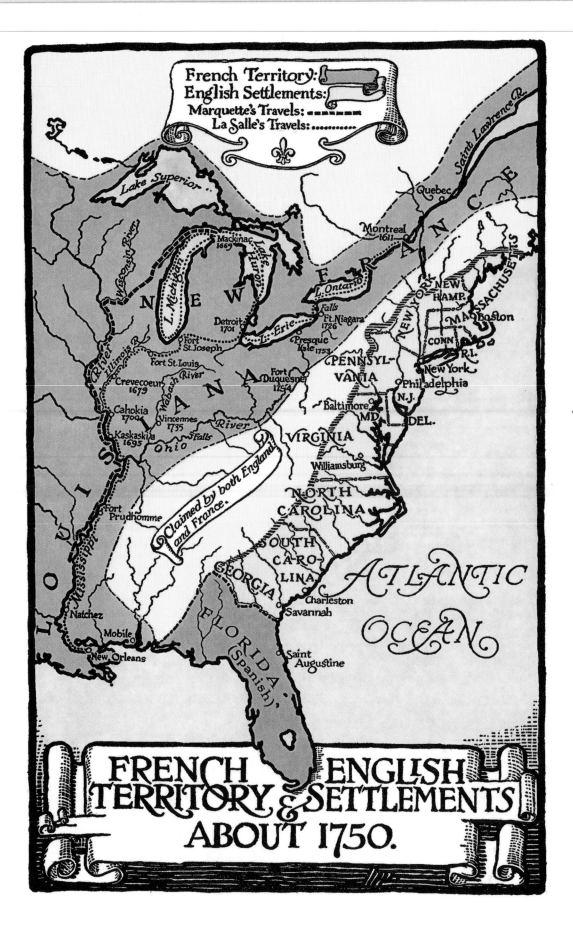

FRENCH TERRITORY & ENGLISH SETTLEMENTS ABOUT 1750.

Pioneers from France

A Story of Traveling by Canoe

Pioneers came to this country from France, as well as from Spain, England, and Holland.

French pioneers sailed up the great river to the north of our country. They named it the St. Lawrence River.

Other French pioneers explored the middle of our land. They found the Great Lakes. They went down the Mississippi River.

The French soon learned to use the Indian birchbark canoes. The canoes were useful boats. They were a fine gift that the Indian gave to the white man. No other kind of boat was so light and yet so strong as the canoe.

Pioneers could take the canoes from the water and carry them from one river to another. They could paddle them in shallow water in small rivers. They could pull the canoes on shore and sleep under them at night.

So French hunters paddled canoes up the rivers. French traders bought canoe loads of furs from the Indians. French priests went by canoe among the Indians to teach them about their religion.

The French treated the Indians well. Most of the Indians liked the French people. They came often to the French towns to trade.

In 1701, a Frenchman started a little town called Detroit. He built a fort and a few houses. His name was Cadillac.

Today, Detroit is a big city. Thousands and thousands of cars are made there each year. Thousands of airplanes are made in the factories. Huge ships bring iron and coal to make the cars and airplanes. Docks line the shore.

It was very different long, long ago when the first white men came to Detroit. Huge trees grew by the water's edge. Wild animals came down to drink. Birchbark canoes slipped quietly through the water.

What was it like, paddling to Detroit in a canoe? The next story, "The Pioneer Doll," will tell you.

The Pioneer Doll

Chapter 13
The Portage

Paddling canoes upstream was hard work! All day the men pushed the canoes forward with their paddles. The canoes carried heavy loads. Marie sat with her mother in the middle of one canoe. Bundles of blankets and clothes, bags of food, axes, and guns were packed carefully around her. She leaned against a big iron kettle for a back.

In her arms, Marie held the most precious thing she owned. It was her doll. It was a beautiful doll. It was dressed in silk and velvet like a queen. It had come from France. Marie called it Lady Claire.

Marie kept the doll well wrapped in a heavy cape. Every now and then she peeked at her. Lady Claire must not get too warm or her wax face and hands might melt. She must not get too cold or they might crack. No water must splash her lovely dress.

Marie held the doll carefully. Then she glanced ahead. The great trees of the forest bent their branches over the water. The canoe swung round a curve in the river.

There, under a giant oak tree, stood a deer drinking! Marie held her breath. The deer was so beautiful. One of the men reached for his gun. A shot rang out. The deer leaped into the air. It ran crashing through the bushes.

The man jumped ashore. Another shot sounded. Then all was still.

"It is such a pity!" sighed Marie's mother. "But we must eat!"

That night they made camp by the riv-

erside. Marie helped her mother cook tender bits of deer meat. They stuck the meat on green sticks and held them over the coals.

It was fun living outdoors when the weather was good. It was fun, except for the mosquitoes! There had been no mosquitoes in France.

"I wish they were all buzzing at the bottom of the sea!" cried Marie.

Her father threw damp leaves on the fire to make smoke to drive them away. But the smoke got in her eyes. Marie gave a sigh. Then she unwrapped the Lady Claire to see if she were dry and safe.

Day after day and week after week, the canoes went on and on. There was one day, though, that Marie would never forget. The canoes had gone as far as they could on the first river. Now the men were going to carry them across to another river. This was their first portage.

The word *portage* means the "carrying." There was plenty of carrying to be done. All morning the men and boys went back and forth carrying loads.

At first, Marie and her mother sat under a great tree by the riverbank. Marie made a garden in a bed of green moss for the Lady Claire. She put ferns and violet plants around her. She made a seat of white stones. There sat the Lady Claire, smiling and lovely.

"I will carry over all the cups and the bowls," said her mother. "Please, see that all the little things are safe."

Then she called to Marie to help her, so Marie followed her down the trail. Their arms were full of many valuable things.

Everything was now across the portage. The men slipped the light canoes into the water and filled them with the loads. The hard work was over.

Suddenly Marie remembered the Lady Claire. She had left her on her mossy throne. Marie turned and ran back down the forest

trail as fast as she could go. No one saw her. Her feet made no sound on the thick leaves. She ran as fast as she could.

Then Marie gave a sigh of relief. There sat her doll. A red leaf had fallen into her lap. Her flowers were fresh and big. She had never looked so lovely.

Suddenly there was a humming sound. A strange tiny bird darted out. Marie had never seen so small a bird. It looked like a jewel with tiny wings. It flew around the Lady Claire. Then it ran its long needle of a bill into the flowers.

Marie stood watching the tiny thing. She had never seen anything like it before.

Suddenly she remembered that she was alone. The forest seemed very big and lonely. She snatched up the Lady Claire. The humming bird darted away. Marie started running back through the woods. She ran wildly along the trail.

Perhaps the others had gone on and left her! Perhaps no one had missed her! Then Marie saw someone coming toward her down the trail. It was her brother Pierre. She started to shout to him. Then she stopped. She would not let him see how frightened she had been. She had been running about like the silly sheep at home. That was how people got lost in the woods.

"I went back to get my doll," she said.

"Why are you carrying her upside down?" asked Pierre.

It was then that Marie saw that she held the lovely Lady Claire with her head down. Her little white kid boots waved in the air.

Quickly she turned the doll right side up! ❏

Chapter 14
The Peace Pipe

When the portage was over, the canoes started downstream. Going downstream was far easier for the men than paddling upstream. The river carried the canoes swiftly along.

But the men who steered the canoes must watch out. The water ran swiftly. There were rocks in the river. The light canoes might strike against one. They might be tipped over or have a big hole torn in the bottom.

Marie sat in the canoe with the Lady Claire in her lap. The doll was smiling and beautiful. Pierre sat in the same canoe near her. Marie told Pierre about the humming

bird. There were many new sights and sounds in this strange land. The first time that Pierre had caught a firefly for her, Marie had thought it would burn her hand.

During the afternoon, rain started to fall. Marie wrapped the Lady Claire in a blanket. Then she pulled a blanket over her own head.

"We had best make camp now," said the men.

But as they turned the canoes toward shore, one of them hit against a sharp point of rock. There was a loud ripping sound. Marie peeked out from her blanket. She could hear shouts. She could see men in the water hanging onto a canoe. Her father paddled swiftly to shore. Then he and Pierre hurried to try to help the other men. But it was too late.

There was a big hole in the canoe. The boat was fast filling with water. Some men managed to save part of the load that the canoe carried. They swam to shore with it. Other men tried to hold up the sinking canoe and pull it to shore.

"What will we do if we lose it?" cried Marie. "The other boats are full already."

"We will have to see," said her mother.

They watched anxiously. The swift, running water was carrying the canoe out of the men's reach. Soon it was lost. The men swam ashore, wet and tired.

"We must get a fire burning to dry them," said Marie's mother.

Everything was soaked. The blanket rolls were wet. The salt bag was wet. There was no need to mix water with the corn meal to make corn bread! The corn meal was wet already.

The men were tired, but they started cutting pine branches to make huts for the night. Marie and her mother worked to get the fire going. It was hard to find dry leaves and twigs.

Pierre took a hatchet to chop open an old log for dry wood. Suddenly he saw something moving in the misty forest. For a moment he stood perfectly still. Then he walked to his father and said in a soft voice, "There are Indians near, I think."

Marie and her mother heard, but they made no sound.

"Keep on with what you are doing," whispered her mother to Marie.

Marie fed chips of wood to the fire. It was hard to hold her hand still. She could not help looking into the misty greenness of the wet forest. Who was there? Who was watching her?

Word that Indians were near went from one man to the next.

"No one is to shoot unless I give the word," said her father softly. He had been among the Indians before. He knew their ways.

Then Marie saw her father take something from a leather bag. It was a long pipe. Feathers, beads, and a wolf's tail hung from it. It was called a peace pipe. Once, long ago, an Indian chief had given it to her father.

Now Marie saw her father hold the pipe above his head. She heard him call out strange words. He was calling to the Indians to come and sit by his campfire. He was inviting them to feast with him.

Pierre threw more wood on the fire. At

last the bright flames blazed up. The fire seemed to warm a little space in the wet, dripping woods.

A tall figure slipped to the fireside. Quietly the tall Indian seated himself. Then came another and another. Marie held her mother's hand, but she stood silently.

The Indians were painted in bright colors. They wore a few feathers in their hair, and strings of bear teeth hung at their necks. As each man came to the fire, Marie's father welcomed him.

"We are your friends," the white man said. "Our fire is your fire."

Fish and deer meat were cooked. The peace pipe was lit and passed from one man to the next.

Then Marie's father told of the lost canoe. He offered blankets and knives and beads for another canoe. He made a pile on the ground and pointed to it.

The chief nodded his head. He had a canoe, a good canoe that he would sell.

Marie's father asked the Indians to go with them to Detroit. There were many Frenchmen in Detroit. They had blankets and knives and kettles and bright little mirrors. They would trade them for furs.

The Indians talked among themselves. They had furs to sell. Yes, they would go with their new white friends. In the morning, they would bring their women and children. They would go to see what the white men had.

As the men talked, Marie sat with her mother in the little hut of pine branches that the men had built. It was open toward the fire.

Marie was growing too sleepy to stay awake any longer. The light from the fire danced against the wet, black forest. It lighted the faces of the Indians. It all seemed like a dream to Marie.

She looked to see that the Lady Claire was warm and dry in her cape. Then Marie's eyes closed and she fell asleep. ❑

Chapter 15
Detroit

In the morning, the woods seemed filled with Indians. Canoes were waiting at the shore. There were Indian women and children with black hair and big dark eyes. They stared at Marie.

The rain had stopped. The sun was shining. Marie stood near the canoe ready to start. She unwrapped the Lady Claire to let her see the world.

An Indian woman saw the doll. She cried out with pleasure. The women and children crowded about the boat. They wanted to pat the soft velvet dress. They wished to look at the tiny boots. They wanted to stroke the doll's hair.

"Let them see Lady Claire," said Marie's mother softly. "I do not think they will hurt her."

Marie held her breath while the Indians passed the doll from one to another. But they were gentle with her. The Lady Claire looked surprised, but she was not hurt. It was strange to see the little French doll with all her fine clothes in the hands of Indian children.

But there was no more time to admire the doll. The canoes were ready to start. There was hurry and excitement. One canoe after another slipped quietly out onto the water. There were twenty of them. Five were filled with French people. The rest carried Indians.

The river grew wider as the canoes moved down it. Then, at last, they came out on a great lake.

"It looks like another ocean!" cried Marie.

Indeed, it seemed almost as large as an

ocean. The canoes kept close to shore.

Sometimes the canoes raced each other. Sometimes the French sang as their paddles rose and fell. It was a grand sight to see so many graceful boats slipping through the water.

Then, one day, the canoes came to the river that led from one great lake to the next. There the little town of Detroit had been started.

"We will be in Detroit before the day is over!" said Pierre.

Suddenly the sky filled with great thunderclouds.

"Oh dear, must it rain again!" sighed Marie.

Thunder roared. Lightning flashed.

"Shall we go ashore?" asked the men.

"Let's keep on," said Marie's father. "We have not far to go."

The rain began to pour down upon them. The canoes kept close to shore so that they could land if they needed to. But no one wished to stop. Detroit was near! Friends were near! Dry houses and warm fires were near!

Suddenly a gun sounded. Marie thought it was more thunder, but it was not. The fort had been sighted. Another gun and another was fired from the canoes. The Indians looked frightened, but the white men pointed joyfully ahead to the fort.

There stood a big fort.

There were log houses nearby. People were running down to the shore. A cannon roared in welcome.

Just as the canoe landed, the rain stopped. The sun came out.

"Look!" cried Marie.

The sun had made a rainbow. It curved in lovely colors across the sky.

"It is a good sign!" cried everyone.

WS

That night it seemed strange to Marie to sleep in a house again. It seemed odd to have a wooden floor under her feet and to be in a dry place when it rained. But soon she was settled and happy in her new home.

The Lady Claire sat safely on a high shelf. She smiled at everyone who came into the cabin. She smiled at the Indians and white people alike.

The Indians stayed for a week at the Frenchmen's fort. They traded their furs. They feasted and they danced around the campfire at night.

At last they were ready to go back to their forest homes. But they promised to come again. They promised to help the Frenchmen and to be their friends.

Just before they left, an Indian woman came to Marie. She smiled at Marie and she held out her hand. What did she have? Marie looked with surprise. What was it? The woman pointed to the Lady Claire.

Then Marie saw what the Indian woman had brought. It was a tiny pair of moccasins. They were made of deerskin as soft as silk. They had tiny beads on their toes. They were lined with the fur of a field mouse. They were moccasins for the Lady Claire.

And so the French pioneers paddled their birchbark canoes on the rivers and lakes in the middle part of our country. Often the French passed by the spot where the city of Chicago stands today. They explored the Great Lakes. They went down the Mississippi River.

Pioneers from France came to live in the central part of our country. Pioneers from Spain came to live in the southern part of our country. Pioneers from England came to live in the eastern part of our country. Pioneers from Holland and from many other lands came to many parts of this land.

How did all these different people become Americans?

How did the United States of America start to be a great country? The next story will tell you. ❏

How Birch Bark Canoes Were Made

1. A tall white birch tree was found. It was chopped down with a stone ax, or a steel ax bought from the white man.

2. The bark was slowly peeled off with wooden wedges. The work must be done carefully. The bark must not be split.

3. A strong frame was made. The wood was soaked in hot water so that it could be bent. Each piece must curve just so.

4. Sticks were driven into the ground to hold the bark in the right shape while the men worked on it.

5. The bark was sewed onto the frame with roots. Roots were tough and strong.

6. Cracks were filled with pitch from pine trees. A canoe must not leak!

7. The canoe was decorated with porcupine quills or paint. When a canoe was done, it was a fine sight to see. It was strong but light.

8. Strong, straight paddles were cut to move the canoe in water. The canoe could move swiftly and quietly through the water. It could carry heavy loads.

Questions

1. What things did the Indians have that the pioneers wanted to buy?

2. What did the French pioneers have that the Indians wanted to buy?

3. Why were birch bark canoes useful?

4. What does the word *portage* mean?

5. Why was it foolish for Marie to "run about like the silly sheep," when she was frightened in the woods?

6. What should you do if you become lost in the woods?

Things to Do

1. Find the St. Lawrence River on the map. Find the Great Lakes and the Mississippi River. What kind of mark is used on a map to show a river? Can you find other rivers on the map?

2. We have read about people from several different countries who came to this country. From what countries did they come? Find out what people were the first to settle near your home.

3. Find the short words in these long words and tell what they mean.

fireside	*campfire*	*Frenchmen*	*rainbow*
deerskin	*downstream*	*upstream*	*riverside*

4. Ask your parents to show you different kinds of fur. Feel the different kinds of fur. Which kind would you use for a baby's cover? Which kind would you use for a man's coat?

5. Dress up a doll to look like Lady Claire.

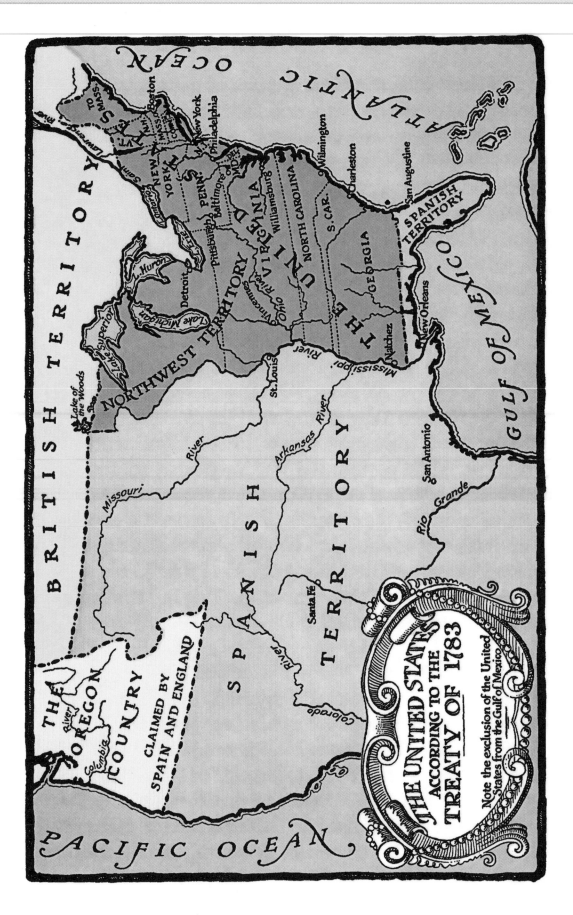

How the United States Began

The Story of a Boy
Who Saw George Washington
Become President

Over two hundred years had now passed since Spanish pioneers had landed in St. Augustine.

Over a hundred and fifty years had passed since Pocahontas saved Captain John Smith.

But still there was no United States of America. There was no flag with red and white stripes, and white stars on blue.

People in the English part of the country began to complain about the laws that England was making. For several years there was talk and trouble. Then a war began between England and some of the people in this country. We call this the War for American Independence.

A great and godly man was put in charge of the American soldiers. His name was George Washington.

The fourth of July is our country's birthday. On that day in 1776, men met together in Philadelphia. They decided that our country should separate from England and be a free country.

There was a big bell hanging in the hall in Philadelphia where the men met. News of what had been decided was told to the people of Philadelphia. The big bell rang out loud and clear. We call this bell the Liberty Bell.

But there was a long and terrible war before our country was free. General Washington led his men through much misery and many hardships. At last, the war ended. Washington and his men won. The English soldiers left this country. The United States was a free land, no longer under the control of England.

At first, the United States was a very small country. There were only thirteen states. Our first flag had thirteen stars on it—one for each state. Today we have fifty states, and fifty great stars on our flag.

When the war ended, our country had no President. At last, it was decided that one must be chosen. There was no question who that man should be. The first President of the United States was to be George Washington.

There was no city of Washington in those days. The city of Washington had not yet been built. So the new President was to live in New York City.

The next story will tell you of the day—April 30, 1789—when Washington was made President.

**The First
President**

Chapter 16
Nathan's Horse

Nathan started off from his home on his horse. The air was cool and sweet with the smell of April flowers. The sun was just rising.

His mother stood at the farmhouse door to wave good-bye.

"Watch out that your horse does not step into a hole," she called. "The road is rocky."

Nathan kissed her good-bye. She looked at the tall, strong boy with pride. Then she said, "I wish your father were alive to see this day!"

Nathan, too, was thinking of his father. He wished with all his heart that his father were riding beside him into New York City to see General George Washington in-

stalled as President.

Nathan's father had been an officer in Washington's army. He had been killed in the War for American Independence.

Nathan had been only a small boy, but he could still remember his father.

"Thud, thud, thud," beat his horse's feet on the dirt road. The geese, chickens, and ducks of the farm were left behind. His dog followed him a little way. It begged to go along, but Nathan sent it back.

The road led through the woods. A rabbit hopped across the road, and birds sang in the trees. It was a lovely time of year.

The horse tried to turn in at a farmhouse, but Nathan kept it on the road. He had no time for calls this day. The horse gave a sigh and trotted on.

Nathan thought of the stories that he had heard of Washington and the war. Often soldiers met to talk. Sometimes they met at the mill where Nathan took wheat to be ground into flour. Sometimes they met at the inn to talk of the old days in the army.

The soldiers talked of the hard, bleak days when it had seemed as though the war would never end. Sometimes there had been nothing to eat. Sometimes men had walked with bleeding feet through the snow because they had no shoes. Through all the hardships, Washington had led them.

Now the war was over. The United States of America was a free country. George Washington was about to become the first President. And Nathan was trotting along on his horse to see the great sight.

New York was a pleasant little town to visit on that bright April day. It was small compared with the New York City of today. It was large, though, when compared with New Amsterdam. Many of the houses were made of brick. They were two or three stories high. There were gardens behind the houses, and trees lined the streets.

Few of the streets were paved. Most streets had holes in them and were muddy when it rained. Pigs wandered here and there. Sometimes a cow ran loose. But this April day was a very special day. Everything in New York was in the best of order.

Flags and strips of bright cloth hung from the windows and balconies. Fine coaches drove through the streets. People wore their best clothes. Ladies had on wide, full skirts and big bonnets. Men wore tight-fitting suits with ruffles of lace. Never had the city looked so magnificent.

Nathan's horse was not sure he liked it all. The waving flags troubled him. He began to dance on his hind legs. But Nathan was a good horseman and rode well. He spoke quietly to the horse and stroked its neck.

Just then a girl leaned out from a balcony. She held a big silk flag. Suddenly a puff of wind blew it out. The horse gave a jump and reared. Then Nathan heard the girl cry out.

The wind had blown the flag from her hands. "Oh, my flag!" she cried. "Someone catch it!"

Down fluttered the big flag. Nathan and his horse were just below the balcony. The flag covered them in a mass of stars and stripes.

The horse gave a jump that nearly sent

Nathan over its head. Then it ran down the street at full gallop. Nathan could hear people screaming and dogs barking. He snatched up the flag with one hand. He waved it as he rode.

People began to clap and to cheer. He could not stop his horse. Around the town he rode waving the flag proudly above his head. At last, the horse was too tired to gallop farther.

The horse's sides were covered with foam. It was panting and trembling. Nathan talked gently to it. Then he rode back to the house where the girl lived.

The same girl was leaning from the balcony. He saw that she was about his age. She had blue eyes and curly dark hair. Nathan handed her the flag.

"Thank you! You were wonderful!" she cried. "At first, I thought the horse would throw you, but when I saw how well you rode, I was not afraid. Thank you for saving my flag."

"Come in and watch the great sights from our windows," said the girl's mother. "We will have a fine view of the balcony where General Washington will stand."

Nathan took his horse to the stable behind the house. He rubbed down its hot sides and left it to rest.

"Come and help me hang out my flag," called the girl, whose name was Abigail. "I sewed every stitch of it myself."

It was a beautiful flag, with its thirteen white stars on the blue background and its red and white stripes. Nathan helped fasten the flag firmly to the balcony so that it could not blow away again. ❑

Chapter 17
The President

A great shout went up from the street. Nathan and Abigail leaned over the railing of the balcony as far as they dared. People were cheering. Boys were throwing their hats in the air. The coach with General Washington had arrived.

"Which man is Washington?" cried Nathan.

"The tall one, the tall one with the white hair," said Abigail.

But it was too late. The men had climbed the steps and gone into the hall. Nathan gave a sigh of disappointment.

"You will see him later," said Abigail's mother.

"He will come out on that balcony. He will stand there when he is made President."

There was a long wait, but Nathan and Abigail had plenty to do. The rooms were filled with people. A cold lunch was laid out with dishes of meats, cakes, puddings, and coffee.

Nathan looked out of the window at the crowds below and above. Windows and roofs were crowded with people. He looked down toward the water at the end of the street. He could see the masts of sailing ships. They were larger ships than the one that had brought Peter and Trinka to New Amsterdam, but they were still sailing ships. As of yet, there were no ocean liners with powerful engines.

At last came sounds of warning. Nathan glanced quickly at the building across the street. Men were coming out on the balcony. Everyone pushed forward to see.

"Careful! Don't fall out!" warned Abigail's mother.

But Nathan was not going to miss seeing George Washington this time!

Out onto the balcony came a group of men. Nathan's heart gave a great jump. There stood Washington! He was taller than the other men. He wore a plain brown suit.

On his head was a white wig tied at the back.

Nathan gazed at the great man. This was the man with whom his father had fought. This was the man who had led his country to liberty.

Washington laid his hand upon the Bible. He was promising to serve his country wisely and well. He was promising to help the United States of America to be a land where people could live in peace and happiness.

Suddenly a

flag was raised over the building. It was the signal. George Washington had become President! Cannons boomed. People cheered and shouted. Again and again the cannons roared. George Washington was President of the United States.

Suddenly Nathan found that a lump was rising in his throat. He could not cheer. He could not shout. Something gripped his heart. Tears were running down his face.

"Do not be ashamed," said Abigail's mother. "This is a great day. It is a solemn day. May God make us all to be worthy of it!"

She wiped her own eyes.

Abigail was calling Nathan to come out onto the street with her. The two ran down the wide stairway. They watched President Washington walk along the street. He was going to St. Paul's chapel on Broadway. He was going to pray for help in the great work before him.

Nathan and Abigail watched the President as he walked through the streets of the little city. He was tall. He was more than six feet. He looked quiet and serious and patient.

He had already done a great work for his country. But there was still much to do. ❏

Chapter 18
The Ride Home

It was evening when Nathan started home on his horse. Abigail leaned from the balcony and waved good-bye to him.

"Come again," she called.

"I'll bring a basket of eggs and fresh butter from the farm," he promised. "And a basket of strawberries."

The road was crowded with people. Now and again fireworks flashed across the sky. Firecrackers and cannons still sounded. Nathan's horse danced along in excitement.

As the boy left the town, he turned to look back. He could see the large red brick house that had been made ready for President Washington. Abigail had told Nathan about it. It was filled with handsome furniture and fine china and shining silver.

There would be many fine dinners and balls given in that house, while President Washington lived there. At night, the ballroom would be lit by hundreds of candles.

Nathan jogged along on his horse. He had seen the man whom his father loved. He had seen a sight that he would never forget. Someday he would tell his children and grandchildren about it. Now he wanted to get home and tell his mother about it.

It was growing dark as Nathan rode through the woods. He and the horse were tired and hungry. Then the horse sniffed the air. He knew he was near home. He began to trot. His hoofs hit a stone and a spark flew out.

At last, a light shone in the window of the little house. Nathan could see someone coming to the door. He called to his mother as he led the horse to the stable.

It was good to sit on the long wooden seat, called a settle, by the fire. The bread, which had been baked that day in the Dutch oven by the fireplace, was warm and fresh. Nathan's mother put milk and cheese and fresh butter on the table.

While Nathan ate, he told his mother of the day. He had much to tell. He could not tell her everything that he had felt. But he told her as much as he could.

It was late when his story was done. The big logs in the fireplace had fallen into ashes. Nathan took out a red coal with a pair of iron tongs. He held it to the wick of a candle and blew on the coal. When the candle was lit, he handed it to his mother. Then he lit a candle for himself.

His mother covered the burning coals in the fireplace with ashes. The two went up the narrow, steep stairs of the little house.

Nathan's mother slept in a high bed with four posts. Dainty white curtains hung about it. Under her bed had been a wonderful place to hide when Nathan was a little boy. Once he had fallen asleep there. His mother had hunted all over the farm, looking for him!

That had been long ago. Nathan was nearly as tall as his mother now. He kissed her good night and went into his own room.

Soon he was asleep. But in his dreams he still saw a tall, serious man with his hand on the Bible. He still heard the cry: "Long live George Washington, President of the United States!" ❏

How People Used Open Fires

1. The fireplace was the most important part of the house. Its fire gave heat and light and cooked the food. A crane held a kettle over the fire.

2. Pothooks held the kettles to the crane. Long pothooks held the kettle in the hot flame, and short pothooks held the kettle farther from the fire.

3. Some iron pots had three legs. They were set in the ashes. When corn bread was baked in one of these, a cover was put on the pot, and hot ashes were piled on top.

4. Meat and turkeys were roasted in an open oven set in front of the fire. A handle turned the rod that held the meat, so that the meat would cook on both sides.

5. Frying pans often had long handles so that people would not have to get too close to the fire. The pans were used for cooking bacon and pancakes.

6. A Dutch oven, built beside the fireplace, was filled with red-hot coals. When it was hot, the coals were brushed out and bread was put in with a long-handled shovel.

7. A warming pan hung by the fireplace. On winter nights, hot coals were put in it. It was used to warm cold beds.

8. Foot stoves were filled with hot coals when people went on trips or sat in cold rooms. Foot stoves were a comfort!

Unit 6 Review

Questions

1. Why do you think our country is called the United States of America?

2. Which state do you live in?

3. What did our first flag look like? How was it different from the flag we have today?

4. Describe some of the things that Nathan saw in New York that Peter would not have seen in New Amsterdam.

5. When the first President was chosen, the story says, "There was no question who that man should be." What does this sentence mean?

6. Where does our President live today?

7. What day is our country's birthday?

Things to Do

1. Find out all you can about George Washington. Perhaps you could invite someone to come and tell you about him.

2. Ask your teacher to help you arrange a bulletin board exhibit. Find pictures of Washington. Find pictures of Mount Vernon, Washington's country home. Find pictures of the city of Washington today.

3. Put up a big sheet of wrapping paper on the wall. Draw a big fireplace on it. On strong cardboard or posterboard, draw several of the things that were used for cooking during Washington's time. Color them, and cut them out. Make a crane that will swing out from the fireplace so that you can lift off the kettles. Make pothooks. Make kettles of different sizes. Make a three-legged kettle.

4. Ask one of your parents to help you make a three-legged stool. You will need three sturdy round wooden poles, a flat circular piece of wood for the seat, and an electric drill for the three holes in the seat. Glue the legs into the bottom side of the seat after you have drilled the proper size holes.

Pioneers Going West

A Story Of Pioneers on the Wilderness Trail

How did our country grow from a little country with thirteen states to a big country with fifty great states?

The first thirteen states were along the Atlantic Ocean. Even before the War for American Independence, people started going west. There was good land beyond the mountains in Kentucky.

It was hard, though, to travel through the forests. Wild animals and Indians were in the woods. There were rivers to cross and no bridges. There also were mountains to find a way through.

There was one famous pioneer named Daniel Boone. He had a gun named "Tick-licker." With his gun in his hand, he explored in the new land of Kentucky.

Kentucky was a fine land. Part of it was covered with thick forest. Part of it was grassland. Buffaloes wandered across it. Deer and game were so thick that a hunter could hit without aiming, so men said!

Daniel Boone marked a trail to Kentucky. He called it the Wilderness Road. It was not really a road, but a path. It was so rough and wild that only people on foot or on horseback could follow it. Part of the Wilderness Road followed an old Indian path. Part of it followed a buffalo trail. At the end of it was a log fort.

Before the American colonies fought England, only a few people came over the Wilderness Road. When the fighting was over, more and more people began to come.

What was it like, going west on this road?

Today you can drive a car where Indians once walked. You can fly in a plane above the weary miles where pioneers walked or rode on horseback.

In some ways, pioneers on the Wilderness Road had an easier time than the first people who came to Jamestown and Plymouth. The men knew how to hunt far better than those first pioneers. The women knew how to make better homes in the wilderness.

In other ways, pioneers going west on this road had a much harder time. No ships came sailing across the sea bringing news and friends from their old homes. When the woods surrounded travelers on the Wilderness Road, they were very much alone.

What was it like, going west on Boone's Wilderness Road? The next story will tell you.

The Wilderness Trail

Chapter 19
The Journey Dress

The Harris family was leaving their home in North Carolina. The corn fields, where Molly, John, and big brother Jed had played hide-and-seek, were also being left behind. Only Baby Susan was too young to remember the old homestead.

"This year we will plant our corn in Kentucky," said Father.

People said that the land in Kentucky was fine and rich. People had talked so much that, here, the whole Harris family was getting ready to leave. Six other families were going, too. They all were going over the Wilderness Road.

"Molly must have a new dress for the journey," her mother said. "It must be of good strong cloth. Surely it will be torn and patched before we reach our new home, so it had better be new from the start."

Molly gave a jump of joy. She had never had a dress that was really new before. Her dresses had always been her mother's old ones, cut down. Now she was to have a new, new dress—a journey dress!

In those days, Molly could not get a dress by just asking for one. No, indeed!

First, Father sheared the sheep. But the sheep did not like it. They baaed and they bleated. Father held them still as the shears went "clip, clip, clip." When the clipping was over, the sheep looked very bare and silly. But a big pile of dirty white wool lay

on the ground.

Next, Molly helped wash the wool. She carried pail after pail of water from the spring. She helped chop wood for a fire to boil the water. Then she scrubbed the wool in it until it was white and clean.

But the journey dress was only just begun!

Next, they carded the wool. But what does carded mean? It means that every bit of straw or burr must be combed out and all the tangles must be straightened. At last, the wool lay in a soft light pile. It was as soft as milkweed fluff.

But the journey dress was not done yet!

Next came the spinning. Round and round went the big spinning wheel. Molly carefully fed in the wool, so that the yarn would be smooth and even. Back and forth she walked. Sometimes a girl walked twenty miles a day as she spun her yarn.

But the journey dress was not done yet!

In the evenings, Molly wound up the yarn. Then it was ready to dye. By the fire stood a dye pot, which had blue dye in it.

"Do not make it too dark a blue," begged Molly.

Her mother dipped the wool, and it came out a beautiful bright blue. Molly clapped her hands with pleasure.

But the journey dress was not done yet!

Mother then worked at the heavy loom. She set it up with linen thread. After that, she wove in the woolen yarn. Linen and wool made stronger cloth than wool alone. It was called linsey-woolsey.

Molly was not strong enough to weave. So she cooked, washed, minded Susan, and cleaned the house while her mother wove. Inch by inch the cloth grew.

"That is the nicest bit of cloth I have ever seen," said Father. "Are you making me a new shirt?"

There was a twinkle in Father's eye, but a sudden fear filled Molly's heart. Perhaps he needed a new shirt more than she needed a dress.

"I have clothes ready for you and the boys," said Mother. "And the shoemaker has made each one of you a new pair of shoes. This cloth is for Molly."

Molly gave a sigh of relief. She was going to have the new dress after all.

Mother spread the beautiful blue cloth on the big table. She cut it with her precious shears. The dress must be long enough so Molly would have room to grow. Mother cut carefully. Then she sewed the dress by hand. The skirt was long and full. The waist was fitted. Molly had to stand still while she tried on her new dress. Next, Father cut wooden buttons to fasten it.

At last, the journey dress was done!

It was a very plain and simple dress, but it was a lovely color. It was just the color of Molly's blue eyes. Her light hair hung down her back in two pigtails. Molly held out the full skirt. She danced across the room. Baby Susan smiled and giggled. Then Father took out his fiddle and played a tune for Molly to dance by.

Molly was ready for the journey. ❑

Chapter 20
The Start

Johnny's new journey suit was made of deerskin. He had shot the deer himself with his father's gun. He had soaked the deerskin in water and scraped off the hair. Then he had put it into a wooden tank of water and hickory bark. Six months it had soaked. This tanned the skin, turning it into leather.

Mother had sewed Johnny's suit. She had made his shirt and trousers, leaving a fringe of deerskin hanging at the sides. She also had made him a coon cap from the fur of a raccoon.

At his waist, Johnny wore a belt with a hunting knife and hatchet hanging from it. But Johnny did not have a gun. He wanted a gun more than anything else in the world.

"Wait till you are fourteen," said his father. "You are big for your age, but you are only twelve."

Every pioneer boy longed for the day when he would have a gun of his own. It meant that he had become a man and could take care of himself. But he must be a good shot before he could have a gun of his own.

There were other things besides guns to think of on this day! The hour for starting on the trip had arrived. Johnny held a packhorse while his father tied on a load.

Small Susan was to ride in a basket tied to one side of a horse. On the other side of the horse was tied a basket for last-minute things.

"Here's the fire kettle, Molly," called her mother. "Put it into the basket. Don't let

it get tipped over."

There were red coals buried in ashes in the little iron kettle. It would be easier to light a fire with the coals than to have to strike a spark with the flint and steel. Of course, after the long day on the trail, everyone would be too tired and hungry to start a fire.

"Don't forget the gourd filled with salt," called Mother.

No indeed, do not forget the precious salt! Salt was hard to get in the wilderness. The men would have to travel many miles to reach the salt springs. Then they would boil away the water, leaving the salt in the bottom of the kettle. So, one of the packhorses carried a huge iron kettle for boiling salt water.

Molly ran back and forth with the few things that remained. Last of all, the spinning wheels were tied on a horse. But the furniture was to be left behind. Father and big brother Jed could make new furniture with their axes. The loom was too heavy to take, as well. But a new one could be made.

The cabin seemed very little and lonely.

"Good-bye, little house," called Molly softly.

A tiny field mouse ran across the floor. It had already moved in.

"Good-bye, little mouse," laughed Molly.

Jed and Johnny were to drive the cow and the sheep. A merry time they had! The cow became frightened by all the strange noises. She ran into the woods, so the boys ran after her. The sheep went in the other direction.

"I'm glad we are not taking a pig," said Mother.

At last, they were off. The cow mooed and the sheep baaed, but the boys drove them down the trail.

They were starting!

Molly looked back at the little cabin and waved good-bye. She was sorry to leave it, but Johnny was glad. He wanted to see buffaloes and wildcats and Indians.

The next day, the Harris family joined other families. The long line of people and animals grew longer. That night they camped by a river. The smell of cooking filled the air. People visited with old friends and made new ones. The children shouted and played.

But as day after day went by, people grew too tired to talk. The trail became rougher and steeper. The men tugged rocks out of the way of the horses and chopped away trees that had fallen across the trail. Then the mountains rose before them.

At the end of the day, people were so tired that they made camp quickly and quietly. Then they dropped to the ground to rest. When they had eaten, they fell asleep.

Jed and Johnny cut their feet on the

rocks. Their new shoes were soon nearly torn to pieces. They had to go barefoot to save them. In the evening, by the campfire, Mother sewed deerskin moccasins for them to wear.

Then one night, Molly woke to hear a shrill cry. Her father jumped to his feet.

He fired his gun. Then all was quiet. But in the morning, some sheep were gone. There was the track of a wildcat in the soft earth.

"Wildcats are the worst beasts of all!" said her father. "They are fierce and they are tricky. Don't ever stop to talk to a wildcat! If you see one, run!"

The cow was thin and tired, but it still gave milk for Susan. Jed milked it each night when they made camp.

"Will we ever get over the mountains?" sighed Molly. ❏

Chapter 21
The Camp

For three weeks, the horses climbed rough trails, passed through valleys, and crossed rivers. Mountains rose on either side of them. On and on and on, the people went. Finally, they passed between the last mountains. Then they started down to Kentucky.

There were many miles still to go and many streams to cross.

"Watch out!" shouted one of the men.

Jed was leading a horse across a stream. Suddenly it slipped on a wet stone. It became frightened. It reared into the air. The heavy pack slipped, and the rope broke. Blankets and bags of food fell into the water.

"Hold on to the horse!" shouted Jed's father.

If the horse started running over the rocks, it would break a leg! Then there would be nothing to do but shoot the poor beast. That would be dreadful.

The horse rolled its eyes in fright and splashed about. But the men got to its head. They quieted the frightened animal and led it through the shallow water to safety.

Jed and Johnny pulled the pack from the water. It was wet and heavy. The women spread out blankets and opened bags of corn to dry.

"We had best camp here for the night," the men said. "It's early, but we need rest."

Men chopped down young trees to make huts for the night. A guard was set to watch the camp. Extra guns were left ready in case of need. Then some of the men went into the woods to hunt for deer or turkey. Food was needed for the weary travelers.

Molly sat under a big tree and played with the baby. She brushed away mosquitoes from Susan's face with a branch. Molly also tickled her baby sister with the tip of the branch and made Susan laugh.

Then Molly smoothed out the skirt of her journey dress and admired it. It had been wet many times. It also was faded and had already been patched, but it was still a pretty color.

Susan grew sleepy, so Molly folded a cloak for her pillow. As she sat beside her, Molly thought of their old home. How far away it seemed! She thought of the new home and wondered what it would be like.

Suddenly a bit of bark fell off a branch above her head. Quickly Molly glanced up. Her heart gave a great jump. She wanted to scream, but she knew better. She sat perfectly still. She was thinking as hard as she could, trying to decide what she should do.

A wildcat crouched on the branch above!

Just then Molly saw Johnny coming down the path. She did not dare move or call out for fear the wildcat would leap onto the baby. Then she gave a low cry, like the cry of an owl. It was a call that she and Johnny often used.

Johnny stopped and looked toward her. Slowly she raised her hand and pointed to the branch. A quick glance revealed to Johnny what was there. He was a pioneer boy, and his eyes were keen. He saw at once that it was a wildcat.

Johnny moved as quietly as an Indian. He picked up one of the guns that stood ready in case of need. It was loaded. He crept silently down the path toward the tree. He aimed the gun at the wildcat.

Molly did not dare breathe. She sat as still as she could. Her eyes were on Susan. The baby was sleeping as peacefully as if she were in her own cradle at home.

Suddenly Johnny fired. The shot rang out through the woods. Susan woke up with a cry, and Molly snatched her in her arms. There was a fierce snarl from the tree. Then there was a heavy thud on the ground.

Men came running from every direction. Women came running, too. What had happened? Indians? Then they saw the big wildcat lying on the ground.

"It's the biggest one I ever saw!" said one man.

"It will make a fine skin for you, Johnny," said another.

But Johnny's father looked at the dead animal carefully.

"That was a good shot, Son," he said. "I guess you have earned a gun of your own."

Johnny's heart gave a leap of happiness. He was to have a gun of his own!

It was two weeks later that the great news came. The fort at the end of the trail was in sight. People hurried along. Shots rang out to tell the people in the fort that a new band of pioneers was arriving.

The big gates of the fort swung open. In went the weary travelers, along with their horses, cows, and sheep. The cows mooed at the scent of other cattle, and the sheep baaed. People laughed and cried and talked all at once.

There was an empty cabin inside the fort. The Harris family could live there until they built a home of their own. At once, Molly began to help her mother build a fire. Soon the kettle was boiling. And Susan was crawling on the floor.

Over the door was nailed a pair of deer horns. They were to hold the guns. They were over the door so that the guns could be snatched down quickly, in case of need.

Johnny stood looking at the horns. Molly stopped what she was doing to stand beside him.

"I'm going to put my gun there," said Johnny proudly.

Now he had a gun of his own! He placed it beside his father's and Jed's.

Then Johnny added, "I'm going to dress the wildcat skin. It will make a fine cover for your bed this winter."

Molly's eyes gleamed. She clapped her hands with delight. Then she held out the skirt of the journey dress, and Father took up his fiddle. In another minute he was playing, and she and Johnny were dancing about the room.

The long trip and the hardships were forgotten. They had a new place to call home. Father gathered the family together for a time of prayer and Bible reading.

Shortly, a new cabin was started in the wilderness. Trees were cut down to build their new home, and corn was planted among the stumps. Molly helped Johnny plant the corn.

What would the pioneers have done without the Indian corn! It would grow in rough ground where wheat would not grow. The ground did not need to be plowed for corn. It was enough to dig a hole with a pointed stick and drop the seed into it.

The Indians' corn was a great gift to the pioneers. ❏

How The Pioneers Made Cloth

1. First the sheep were sheared. The thick wool was cut off. The sheep looked silly and bare, but new wool soon grew.

2. Then the thick, heavy wool had to be washed. Grease had to be washed out. Sticks and burrs had to be picked out.

3. Next the wool was carded. The cards were boards with sharp nails sticking out from them. The nails pulled the wool apart and combed it.

4. When the wool was carded, it was soft and fluffy. Next it had to be spun into yarn. Round and round went the big spinning wheel.

5. Then the yarn was wound on a clock reel. Next the dye was made in the big dye kettle. Brown dye was made from the bark of hickory trees.

6. The wool was dipped into the dye. Then it was hung up to dry. At last, it was ready to knit into stockings, or to weave into cloth.

7. Cloth was woven on a loom. Linen thread and woolen yarn were woven together to make linsey-woolsey cloth. It was stout and strong and warm.

8. When the cloth was done, then came the question, "Who needed it most?" Mary needed a dress. Father needed shirts. There was never enough to go round.

Unit 7 Review

Questions

1. What was the name of the trail over the mountains and through the mountains that went into Kentucky?

2. What was the name of the man who marked out the Wilderness Trail?

3. Do you know how trails are marked through the woods? Have you ever followed a trail in the woods?

4. What things do you think a man would have to take with him to stay alive for many days in the woods?

5. How did Molly get her journey dress?

6. How did Johnny get his first gun?

7. Why was Indian corn more useful to the pioneers than wheat?

Things to Do

1. When the pioneers started going west to Kentucky, they had to go over mountains and through mountain passes. Ask your teacher the name of those mountains. See how mountains are marked on a map.

2. Draw a picture of something that happened in this story. Hold it up and choose someone to tell what the scene is.

3. Find four things in your home that are made from leather.

4. Draw a picture or find a picture of a spinning wheel. Explain how a spinning wheel works.

Going West by Water

A Story of Pioneers on the Ohio River

Some pioneers went west by water. They built flatboats and loaded all their things on them. The river carried the flatboats along. These pioneers floated downstream in search of new land to start a fresh life.

But floating downstream could be dangerous. At times, a boat could run against rocks and be broken to pieces. Other times, dead trees were stuck in the river. These trees could tear a hole in the bottom of a boat. Sand bars also lay hidden just under the water, and a boat could be stuck on a sand bar. In addition, Indians, or Native Americans, might paddle out from shore and attack.

As time went by, the Indians became more fierce and angry. They saw that the settlers were taking more and more of their land. The settlers were killing the deer and buffaloes. They were cutting and burning down the forests. They were taking away the Indian's food and homes.

Some of the settlers were fair and honest. They paid the Indians for the land. They lived alongside the Native Americans and learned their ways.

But other settlers were greedy. They broke their promises. They stole from the red men, burned their villages, and killed their wives and children. Many Indians began to hate all European settlers.

It was sad that the wisest settlers and the wisest Indians did not meet to decide where the settlers should live and where the Indians should live. It was sad that the settlers often did not keep their promises to the Native Americans.

The Ohio River is a wide, deep river that flows west through our land. Many thousands of pioneers went down the Ohio River in flatboats.

Little towns were started along the river. In these towns, people could buy what they needed for the trip. Families with horses and cows and food were loaded onto big flatboats. Then off the boats floated.

What was it like going west on the Ohio River? The next story will tell you.

The O'Neil Family Goes West

Chapter 22
The O'Neil Family

There were eight children in the O'Neil family. They went, all the way, from big brother Joe, who was six feet tall, down to Baby Betsy, who was only as big as a picnic basket.

The O'Neils were going west. Mother gave a sigh. Again she was packing up the quilts and blankets, the kettles and frying pans, the spinning wheels and butter churn. Father had his guns and ax, his shovel and hoe, his box of tools, and his seed corn.

It was the third time that the family had moved west. When the children sat by the fire in the evening, Mother used to tell about the moves.

"I was born back East in Boston," Mother would begin. "That is a fine town. It has fine houses and stores and inns, and it has more people than you could count. When I married, we went to a farm in Connecticut. I made my first journey by sleigh, for it was winter. It was fun, dashing over the snow with a pair of fast horses.

"We put hot bricks in the bottom of the sleigh to keep our feet warm. We carried along a big chunk of bean porridge all cooked and frozen stiff. We would break off a piece to eat. You know the rhyme,

Bean porridge hot, bean porridge cold,
Bean porridge in the pot, nine days old!"

Mother stopped to turn the heel on the sock that she was knitting. The children listened with eyes wide open. Cities!

Farms! Sleighs! They had been brought up in the woods. But back East, there were cities and towns and roads. Mother had seen them all.

On went the story. "But your father was restless. He said there were too many people in Connecticut. So we moved into New York State. This time we went by stagecoach.

"Oh, a stagecoach is a fine way to travel! But sometimes the stagecoach got stuck. Once it almost turned over. I let out such a scream that everyone thought I was killed. Joe was just a baby then."

The children looked at big brother Joe, six feet tall. It was funny to think of him as a baby, riding in a stagecoach.

"Finally, we reached our next home," said Mother. "It was wild country, all woods and Indians. But pretty soon, your father began talking about moving again—this time into Pennsylvania. That was even wilder than the country we had left behind. Not a road to drive on, or an inn to stay at. No more stagecoaches!

"We started out in an oxcart pulled by six oxen. Sometimes the trail was so narrow that your father had to chop down trees to get the cart through. The cart could be heard five miles off, banging over rocks. It was lonely in the forest at night. A bear stole my bacon! Wolves howled!"

Mother stopped again to count the stitches in her knitting. Then she said slowly, "Now we are moving again, this time into Indiana. We are going down the Ohio River in a flatboat."

Mother gave a sigh. "Each time I leave a place, I always take a root from my rose bush and a root from my lilac bush with me in a pot," she said. "The first ones came from my old home in Boston. Everywhere I've lived, I have had roses and lilacs. I always was a great one for flowers."

Each older O'Neil child had a younger one to care for on the journey. Eight-year-old Mary Jane had charge of Davy, who was two. He kept her busy. At the present, he was falling headfirst into the flatboat that was to carry them down the Ohio River.

Mary Jane grabbed Davy by the back of his homespun dress. Then she helped her older sister Martha carry Baby Betsy down.

Mary Jane peeked into the cabin of the boat. "It's just like a playhouse!" she cried.

But it was far from being a playhouse! The walls were of thick planks. The windows were narrow slits. It was a fort, as well as a house. No bullets or arrows could go through those thick walls.

The girls spread out big quilts and blankets. They unpacked pewter dishes and wooden bowls.

Just then, there came a great noise from the deck. The girls ran out to see what was happening. The boys were driving the horses and mules, the cows and pigs, and the sheep aboard. One of the pigs got away, and the boys had to chase it.

Suddenly, Mary Jane saw a strange old man standing by the boat. He was dressed in rags. His hair and beard were long.

"You had better not talk to him," whispered Martha. "He looks strange."

But the old man smiled at Mary Jane. He smiled in a way that made her forget that she was afraid. She smiled back.

"Here is something for you, little girl," he said, and he gave her a little bag.

"There are seeds in there," said the old man. "Apple seeds. Plant them by your new home, and someday you will have nice young trees. Every child should have apple trees to climb and apples to eat."

"Thank you," said Mary Jane. "Thank you very much."

She ran to her mother with the seeds.

"That's a fine idea! " said her mother. "It was kind of the old man. He must be

Johnny Appleseed. He goes about giving people seeds and tending young trees, so the new places won't seem so lonely. I wish I had an extra rose bush to give him."

"He was poor and ragged," said Mary Jane.

"Don't judge people by their looks," said her mother. "He spends his time and money doing kind things for people. There are plenty of people that bless his name."

Mary Jane looked at the little brown seeds. They were more than apple seeds, she thought. They were seeds of kindness. It would be wonderful to have apple trees by their new home. ❏

Chapter 23
On the Ohio

The next day, the O'Neil family started off. There were three other men on board. One man had his wife and baby. The boat was well filled with people and animals. It was like a floating farm. Out into the broad river, it floated quietly.

One person stood on the roof of the cabin and steered with a long oar. The boys and men took turns steering. The women cooked and knitted and washed and cared for the babies. There was time for talking and fun, as well.

When the boat floated past log houses, the children waved to the people ashore. But sometimes, day after day went by with no sign of people or houses. The woods came down to the water on either side. It was fall, and the leaves were turning red and gold.

Best of all, Mary Jane liked to have one of the men take out his fiddle. Then they would all sing and dance. She would beg for "Old Dan Tucker," and they would sing:

"Old Dan Tucker was a fine old man.
He washed his face with a frying pan.
He combed his hair with a wagon wheel.
And died with a toothache in his heel!"

One night, as they sat on deck—singing and laughing—a light flamed in the sky ahead.

"Is it a forest fire?" asked Joe.

"I don't think it is," said his father slowly. Then he added, "I don't like the looks of it."

In less time than it takes to tell, the lanterns on board were put out. The little children were hurriedly tucked away in the bunks. Men stood at the window slits with their guns. Silently they watched the light ahead.

Mary Jane could see the light from a window. There were clouds over the stars. No moon shone.

In the darkness of the night, the heavy boat floated on and on. For there is no way to stop a flatboat, except to run it ashore. And there is no way to hurry a flatboat. It floats slowly or fast, as the river runs.

Brother Joe stood at the steering oar.

"Keep as near the bank as you dare," said his father in a low voice. "Steer close to the far shore. But watch out! Don't get us stuck on a sand bar!"

The heavy dark boat swung round the curve in the river. Suddenly, strange sounds filled the air. Shouts and yells rang across the water. It was easy to see from where the sounds came. A huge fire burned near the bank of the river. Dark figures danced about it.

"Indians!" whispered Mr. O'Neil. "It's a war dance!"

The fire made a path of light across the

dark water. Slowly, but steadily, the flatboat floated toward the light.

Mother leaned over Mary Jane and whispered to her, "Keep Davy quiet. If Father calls, wrap Davy in a quilt and bring him out on deck. Be ready to do just what Father says, and don't make a sound!"

Nearer and nearer to the light floated the flatboat. The cries and shouts of the dancers grew louder and louder. The warriors leaped around the fire and waved war clubs in the air. Boom, boom, boom, went the beat of the big war drums. It seemed to Mary Jane as though her heart was beating as fiercely as the drums.

Would the Indians see the boat as it floated quietly past? Would the darkness hide it?

"No one is to fire a gun unless I give the word," whispered Mr. O'Neil.

Baby Betsy turned in her sleep and gave a little cry. Martha bent over her. She sang softly to her. The baby gave a sigh and was quiet.

Mary Jane sat by Davy. He was asleep now. She thought of Joe on the roof of the cabin steering the boat. Oh, if only he could push the boat along faster with that big oar! Oh, how she wished he could push them past the light and into the darkness beyond!

The Indians were busy with their dance. The chief was telling how the European settlers had taken their hunting grounds and killed their deer. He was telling how they had burned the forests. As he spoke, the warriors stopped to listen. Then the wild dance began again.

On and on floated the silent boat. Then slowly, it floated into the light from the fire. But the Indians were so busy with their dance that they did not see it. Suddenly, one Indian looked toward the water.

The Indian gave a great shout. The drums stopped. Dark figures came leaping down the bank of the river. Arrows flew through the air. Canoes were pushed into the water.

"No one is to shoot unless an Indian gets close enough to climb on board," ordered Mr. O'Neil firmly.

Bullets hit the flatboat, too. The Native Americans had bought guns from the settlers. So now, some had guns, as well as bows and arrows. But the bullets did not pierce the thick sides of the boat.

On and on the flatboat floated, into the safe darkness of the night. At last, the Indian canoes turned back. The cries grew fainter. Then the drums began again.

It was then that Mary Jane found that she wanted to cry. She threw herself into her mother's arms.

"Cry all you want to now, Dearie," said her mother. "You were quiet and brave when there was danger. That's the important thing!"

Just then something happened that made Mary Jane forget herself. The men came in carrying brother Joe. A bullet had hit him. He had been shot as he stood at the steering oar. He had not cried out. His screams would have told the Indians where the boat was. He had stood bravely at his work till the danger was past. ❑

Chapter 24
The New Home

Everyone was glad when they reached the new home. Joe was better, but he still lay white and quiet in his bunk. Mary Jane ran in and out of the cabin to bring him the news. The flatboat was tied up at the shore near a little town of log houses. Father had bought land, and the men were starting to build a log cabin.

It took a week to build the new log house. The three men who had come down the river with the O'Neils paid for the trip by helping. Seventy or eighty straight tall pine trees were cut. The trunks were sawed to the right length. The ends were cut so that they fitted together. It was hard, heavy work, but the log walls were thick and strong. No bullet or arrow could go through them. Winter wind and snow could not get in either, for the cracks were filled with clay and mud.

At last, Mary Jane ran to the flatboat to tell Joe the news. The house was done. The front door was hung on leather hinges. A wooden latch held it shut.

The furniture was soon made. The table was made of a rough slab of wood set on four posts. The posts were fitted into holes bored in the floor. Also, short posts were made to hold up the rough beds. Ropes were then stretched across to hold the bags of hay that were used for mattresses. Finally, bear-skins and blankets were spread over them.

It was an exciting day when the O'Neil family moved into the new house. Mother cooked bear meat over the open fire. Martha made "hasty pudding" of corn meal. It was called "hasty pudding" because it could be made so fast. The corn meal was boiled in water. Then molasses was poured over it.

The flatboat was taken apart, as well. It was too heavy to push back up the river. The planks would make a fine barn for the animals.

"The girls ought to go to school this winter," said Mr. O'Neil, as they sat down to the first dinner. "I need the boys to cut trees and split rails for fences. But the girls can have some schooling. There is a school started in town."

Martha and Mary Jane looked at each other in surprise—school! They had never been to school! They had learned to read from their mother, who taught them to read from the Bible. They could write their names, but that was about all. What would it be like at a country school?

The next day, the girls took Davy and walked past the open door of the school. They peeked in. The schoolhouse was a log cabin. The children sat on benches with no backs. The schoolteacher sat at a high desk.

On his desk, he had a big pen made from a feather. He looked very solemn.

The youngest children stood in front of him. They were reading.

"A, b, ab," said one child slowly. "E, b, eb."

It did not sound interesting to Mary Jane. Then one boy at the back of the room pinched another boy. The schoolmaster

shouted at him and rapped on his desk with a cane. Mary Jane gave a jump and Davy began to cry. The girls hurried home.

"Couldn't we wait till next year to begin school?" they begged.

"I'll help with the spinning," said Martha.

"I'll help with the soap making and the candle dipping," said Mary Jane.

"I'll help churn the butter," said Martha.

"I'll pound the corn into meal and bake the bread," said Mary Jane.

"Well, well," laughed Mother. "I really don't see how I could get along without you! You can wait until next year if you will read from the Bible to me every night and sew on your samplers every day."

So every day, when the housework was done, the girls sewed on their samplers. Every evening they sat by the open fire and read to their mother. They also worked on

their arithmetic lessons.

How warm and comforting that fire was! The log in back was so big that a horse had to drag it into the kitchen. Then Joe and his father rolled it into the fireplace.

Sometimes the big back log burned for weeks. Mother piled smaller wood on top of it. How warm and comforting the fire was! It was good to sit by the fire after a long day's work.

There was so much to be done!

"I wish we each had three pairs of hands," said Father.

All winter the boys and men worked. They cut down trees to build fences so that the cows would not stray into the woods and be killed by the wolves and bears. They also cleared land to plant in the spring.

When warm weather finally came, the planting of corn, wheat, and oats began. Mother and the girls started a garden. Beans and potatoes were planted.

"I hope the bears won't eat the ears of corn, and the deer won't eat everything else!" sighed Mother.

She planted her rose and lilac bushes by the cabin door.

"I want to plant my apple seeds," said Mary Jane.

Father found a good place and dug up the ground for her. Mary Jane planted the seeds in a row. Then she built a fence around them to keep out the chickens. She watched for the tiny shoots to come up.

"If Johnny Appleseed ever comes this way," said Mary Jane, "he'll be pleased with my apple trees."

"It will be a long time before those bear fruit," said Martha.

"I can wait," said Mary Jane. ❑

What Pioneer Schools Were Like

1. The schoolhouse was a log cabin with a fireplace to heat it. The children who sat near the fire in winter were too hot. The others were too cold.

2. The smallest children learned from a hornbook. It was a board with large and small letters pasted on. A thin sheet of cow's horn kept it clean.

3. After the hornbook, the children read the Bible or the New England Primer. This is a page from the New England Primer.

4. Next came the spelling book. Every school had spelling matches. Even grown-ups had spelling matches.

A pen knife
Quill
Sand   Inkwell

5. Children wrote with quill pens made from feathers. The teacher cut the ends of the quill with a sharp knife. It was called a penknife.

6. Paper was hard to get, so most of the work was done on slates. Slates were thin sheets of stone. They could be washed. Slate pencils often squeaked.

A sampler

7. Little girls often learned their letters by sewing them on samplers. This is a picture of a sampler.

8. The teacher always had a paddle for naughty children. Any child who would not learn sat in the corner.

Questions

1. Do you think it was easier for pioneers to go west by land or by water? Why?

2. Why were the Indians becoming more fierce and angry? What do we wish the wisest Indians and the wisest settlers had done?

3. What did Mother take west with her? What did Father take? Make a list of these things. Which three things do you think were the most important? Why?

4. Mr. O'Neil said, "I wish we each had three pairs of hands." Why do you think he said that?

5. What is pewter? Why would dishes of pewter or wood be better than china for the pioneers?

6. What books did the children read in home schools or in the local pioneer schools?

Things to Do

1. Find the Ohio River on a map of the United States. Where does it begin? Into what large river does it flow?

2. Mother had moved from the city of Boston to Connecticut and then to New York State. She then moved on to Pennsylvania, and out to Indiana. Find those states on the map. Trace with your finger where Mrs. O'Neil traveled during her lifetime, starting from Boston, Massachusetts.

3. Arrange a bulletin board or poster board with pictures of the different ways by which the pioneers traveled.

4. Ask your parents if you can plant an apple tree.

5. Bring a feather to class. Ask your teacher to cut the end in a point to make a quill-like pen. If you have a bottle of ink, dip the tip of the quill in the ink and sign your name.

Going West by Wagon Train

A Story of Pioneers Traveling by Covered Wagon

West, west, west, went the pioneers. They crossed the Mississippi River in boats. They came to the wide prairie where the buffaloes lived. Some pioneers made their homes there. Other pioneers kept on going further west toward California.

After the prairies were crossed, there came the plains. Then, far ahead, rose great mountains. First came the Rocky Mountains. Then, for a thousand miles, there were deserts and mountains to be crossed.

In many places, the trails through the mountains were steep and dangerous. In summer, as well as in winter, there was snow on the white peaks. Storms blew down the trails.

In the desert, the sun beat down. Often there was no water or grass. Many oxen and mules died.

People threw away things to make wagons lighter. Piles of furniture, stoves, trunks, cooking things, and food were left behind. There was nothing else to do.

The way was marked by graves of people who had died. Still the pioneers struggled on.

Many pioneers traveled in covered wagons. These wagons were painted blue with red trimming. The ends were higher than the middle part so that babies and bundles would not fall out. The wagons could bump over rocks and down into mud holes.

If rivers were too deep to wade across, the wheels of the wagon were taken off. The wagon box was like a boat. It was rowed across the water or pulled by ropes. The animals swam.

It was a big sight to see a long line of covered wagons starting out from the old French city of St. Louis. The line was called a wagon train. It was safer to travel in a wagon train than alone. Sometimes two or three hundred wagons set out together. Twenty miles was a good day's trip.

It was not so happy a sight as the weeks went by. Colors faded in the sun and wind. Wheels were broken on rocks. People were scruffy and weary, and wagons were worn and battered.

Sometimes men struggled for hours to drag one wagon after another up a steep cliff. Every so often, it took fifteen oxen to pull each wagon across a stream, as well.

At times Indians attacked, but at other times Indians helped. They saved many lives. They led to safety many parties of pioneers who were lost.

What was it like going west in a covered wagon? The next story will tell you.

"Catch Up! Catch Up!"

Chapter 25
The Wide Prairie

By four o'clock in the morning, everyone was up. Dogs barked and cows mooed. Babies cried, and women called to the children. Men shouted at the oxen and horses, because they had turned the animals loose to graze for an hour before starting.

A hundred wagons stood in a huge circle. Inside the circle, the women were building fires and cooking food. By sunrise, the wagon train must be ready to start.

"Hurry up, Dan!" called his sister. "Finish your breakfast fast! Pack the dishes for me."

"Hurry up, Dan!" cried his father. "Help me with these oxen!"

"Hurry up, Dan!" called his mother. "Lift this tent into the wagon!"

Dan gave a groan. All was hurry and noise. It was always this way the first thing in the morning. Everybody wanted him to do everything at once.

Soon would come the call, "Catch up! Catch up!" At that call, the first wagon would start out. The second and third would fall into line.

But today was to be different.

As Dan sat eating his breakfast, he felt the ground shake under him. He put his ear down to listen.

"I hear something coming," he called to his father.

His father bent over to listen. "Thud, thud, thud," came the sound of heavy hoofs on the earth.

"Indians?" asked Dan.

"Too loud," said his father. "It sounds more like buffaloes."

He called quickly to some men. They saddled their horses and rode off. Dan jumped on a horse and followed his father. They galloped to a low hill. They stopped and looked out over miles and miles of rolling prairie.

Far away Dan could see a cloud of dust moving toward them. Nearer and nearer it came. At last, he could make out a mass of buffaloes. They came thundering across the prairie toward the camp. Something

had frightened them.

"We must keep them away from the wagons," shouted Dan's father. A herd of buffaloes could wreck a whole camp.

The men spread out across the prairie. They must drive the herd in another direction. The horses were excited and nervous.

"Keep close to me, Dan," shouted his father.

On and on came the herd. The ground shook under the beat of their hoofs. But the buffaloes were stupid animals. They seemed to pay little attention to where they went.

One man rode forward. Suddenly, a big buffalo saw him. The buffalo stopped and looked. It was curious about this stranger. Dan could see the small horns sticking out. He could see the small red eyes.

The man fired. There came a roar from the buffalo. The beast was wounded. It stamped the ground with its sharp hoofs. Its long tongue hung from its mouth. Then, with a roar, it dashed forward. Straight toward Dan, the buffalo came!

For a second, Dan's horse stood still, trembling. The buffalo was almost upon them. Then the horse gave a quick jump to one side. Dan almost went over its head. He clung to its neck. The buffalo went dashing past. Dan's horse galloped to safety.

Another man aimed his heavy gun and fired. The buffalo fell to the ground. It was dead.

Dan slipped back into his saddle. Then he quieted his frightened horse. That jump had saved his life. He patted the horse's neck.

A second and a third buffalo were killed. Then the herd turned. It galloped off in another direction, away from the wagons. For now, the camp was safe. The men followed the herd for a while. They killed as many buffaloes as they could.

It was noon when the party got back to camp. The sun was hot. Dan was tired, but there was no rest in camp. The mules and oxen had been filled with terror at the noise. They had broken loose and scattered far and wide across the prairie.

"It will be work, rounding them up," said Dan's father. "We had best stay right here for a few days. It's a good time to dry buffalo meat to take with us."

All that afternoon and the next day, Dan and the boys rode across the prairie. They hunted for the lost oxen and tried to catch the runaway mules. In some places, the buffalo grass grew as tall

as a horse's back. Here and there, patches of sunflowers bloomed. Prairie dogs sat up on their hind legs and barked at the boys. Dan rode near them, but they dove down into their holes.

Some of the men cut up the buffalo meat. They hung it in the sun to dry. It was well to have dried meat on hand.

Three days later, the cry "Catch up! Catch up!" came again. All but three of the lost animals had been found. The train was ready to start.

At sunrise, the barking, shouting, and mooing began. After that, the creaking of wagon wheels was heard. Tents were down. Kettles and frying pans were packed. Bedding and buffalo robes were rolled up.

Slowly the long line of wagons moved across the prairie. It looked like a long line of crawling ants. Dust filled the air. Dan and his father walked by the side of the wagon. His mother and sister rode. The day's march had begun. ❏

Chapter 26
Mountains and Desert

Little by little, the trail began to rise. The rich prairie land was left behind. Ahead, mountains loomed against the sky. The trail became so rough that the wagons bumped and groaned.

Every night there were wagon wheels to mend. Iron rims were made tight by hammering in wooden wedges. The rough going was pounding the wheels to bits. When an ox died, its skin was used to make strong straps to tie up weak wheels.

"Watch out for rattlesnakes," warned Dan's father, as they made camp at night.

Wolves and coyotes howled around the wagons. The stars were bright and beautiful, as Dan lay and looked up at them.

One evening, Dan and his father rode away from camp looking for game. Fresh meat would taste good. They rode up a strange, wild valley. Dan watched eagerly for any sign of game. Perhaps he would see a deer.

Suddenly he saw something that made him stop his horse. Ahead was a large covered wagon. It was tipped sideways. One wheel was broken. In front of it lay two dead oxen. Big black birds called vultures whirled in the air above it.

Dan looked at his father. They had seen many broken-down wagons along the way. They also had seen many oxen, mules, and horses that had died beside the long, hard trail. But this wagon looked so lonely and so helpless!

Dan's father fired at the vultures to frighten them away. They were fierce and greedy. They flapped their great wings and flew away. Then Dan and his father rode toward the wagon.

They called and shouted, but there was no answer. The horses did not like the sight. They rolled their eyes and tried to run back.

"I don't believe there's anyone there, but you'd better see," called Dan's father.

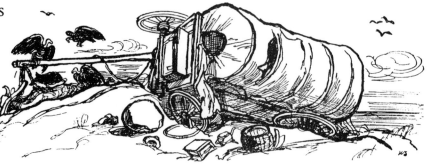

Clothes, bedding, and kettles had tumbled out of the wagon as it tipped. The oxen had dragged it behind them as they looked for water. They had gone as far as they could before they dropped to the ground.

"Somebody has had a mighty hard time," said Dan.

His father looked very sober. Without a doubt this might happen to any of them.

Just then Dan heard a strange sound.

Was it an animal or a bird? A little sobbing sound came from the wagon. Dan jumped from his horse.

"Go carefully there," Father warned him.

Dan crept up to the wagon. Then he climbed up on one of the big wheels and peeked under the cover. The little cry came again.

"There's somebody in here!" he shouted.

There in a basket lay a baby girl. She was very thin and was sobbing softly. Dan picked her up and climbed out of the wagon. She clung to him.

His father looked down at the baby.

"Well, this is a pretty funny hunt we came on," he said. "I didn't know we were baby hunting. Wrap her up in something."

Dan pulled a small quilt from the wagon. Then he held the baby up, and his father gently took her in his arms.

"Poor little thing," he said. "Her father and mother must have left the wagon to look for help. Wonder what happened to them. Shot by Indians perhaps. Another day and this baby would have been dead. Thank the good Lord we came along."

When they reached camp, the women crowded around to see the baby. She was dressed in a neat linsey-woolsey dress of dark blue. She had on a little blue-and-white checked apron. Dan's mother heated milk for her. Then she fed the tiny girl a drop at a time. After that, Dan's sister held her in her arms, tenderly rocking the baby back and forth.

The next morning, the men rode back to the broken-down wagon. They hunted and looked, but there was no sign of its owners.

"I'll keep the baby," said Dan's mother. "I've been wanting a baby."

It was surprising how fast the baby gained weight. In a few days, she grew stronger. When Dan came near, she laughed and smiled. She was loved and cared for, but she knew nothing of what had happened. ❏

Chapter 27
The Lost Trail

Dan woke up one morning to find everything white. His buffalo robe was frozen to the ground. He was stiff and cold.

"We can't go on today," said his father in an anxious voice. "We might lose the trail."

"Lose the trail!" thought Dan. Those were words that filled every pioneer's heart with fear.

Getting a fire started was hard. Dan crawled under a wagon to find a dry spot. His hands ached with the cold. At last, he got a small fire going. It was good to smell the wood smoke. At once, his mother cooked hasty pudding and warmed milk for the baby.

All that day, people lay inside tents and wagons trying to keep warm. They wrapped themselves with buffalo robes. But the cold made it hard to keep the children quiet. Also, the dogs howled; and the long, mournful cry of a wolf was sometimes heard. All day snow and rain fell.

Next morning, the men gathered together. They looked at the sky and talked. The snow had stopped, but the sky was gray. The men were anxious and troubled. Could they find the trail with snow on the ground? At last, the word was given for the wagon train to start.

It was a quiet starting this time, but it was good to have something to do. Dan hurried to help. He did not have to be called.

A party of men rode on ahead to be sure of the trail. Dan's father led them.

"You drive the oxen, Dan," he called.

Dan took the long whip and led the beasts. They moved along slowly. The oxen slipped on the wet rocks.

Then one wagon ahead broke down. A wheel was gone. The men hurried forward and pulled it out of the way. The wagon would have to be left. A few things could be saved and piled into another wagon,

but the rest must be left behind.

The woman and the children from the broken wagon sadly moved in with friends. The man walked, as the long line moved on again.

By noon, the whole train stopped. It had begun to rain again. Then the men who had ridden ahead came back. They brought bad news. They spoke quietly, but their eyes looked worried and afraid.

"We've lost the trail," they said.

"Lost the trail!" the people gasped. They looked at each other in terror. What would happen now? What could they do, lost in the mountains? Who was there to help them?

Suddenly, out of the storm, came two men on horseback. Two tall Indians rode toward the wagons. They sat straight and tall on their Indian ponies.

Men jumped up and reached for their guns. Children hurried to their mothers. They watched the Indians with eyes big with fear. What were they going to do?

The leader of the Indians made a sign. It was a sign of peace. Dan's father hurried forward. He gave a great sigh of relief. He shook hands with the Native Americans. He made them welcome.

There was little to offer the Indians. Dan's father led them to a dry spot by a wagon. Dan spread a buffalo robe for them to sit upon. His mother brought them food.

For some time, the Indians sat quietly eating. Dan looked at them eagerly. One must be a great chief. He wore a fine deerskin suit. He had a buffalo robe over his shoulders. Around his neck hung strings of bear claws. Both Indians had guns.

One Indian spoke a little English. When he had finished eating he took out a pipe. He filled it with tobacco. It was a peace pipe.

"Smoke," said the Indian. Settler and Indian smoked the pipe of peace together.

Dan's father told the Indians that the wagon train had lost the trail. He asked for their help.

One Indian nodded his head slowly. After that, he spoke to the other man.

Then he said quietly, "We show trail."

They must start at once. The rain

wagons through?"

The Indians rode on ahead. They knew these mountains. This was their home.

By evening, the wagons were back on the trail. People talked and laughed as they made camp. They were cold and wet, but they were safe. They had found the trail.

Dan's father called to him. "We must give presents to the Indians," he said.

The Indians liked the settler's clothes. Dan's father chose two fine coats and hats. Then he picked out a roll of red cloth and a package of red powder to mix into paint. Was that enough? Would the Indians be pleased?

He added beads and little mirrors for them to take to the women.

With his father at his side, Dan carried the presents to the Indians. Solemnly the two men took them. As they started to climb onto their horses, Dan stepped forward. He took out his hunting knife, which he always wore at his belt. He held it out to the Indian chief.

"This is for your son," Dan said.

Solemnly the chief took the knife. He put it in his belt. Then he took the long string of bear claws and put it around Dan's neck.

"My son and you, brothers," he said.

Then the Indians rode quietly away.

It is true that Almighty God works in strange ways to protect people from harm. Only God can make people who are often enemies to live at peace with one another. ❏

would swell the rivers. The wagons might not be able to get across. There was no time to lose.

As they started through the wet snow, big wheels began to creak and groan. But there was a different feeling inside the wagons. Instead of being frightened and lost, people were happy and excited.

The Indians were helping them to find the trail. The Indians knew the way. Through a narrow rocky pass, the Indians led the line of wagons. The mountains rose like steep walls on either side.

"We would never have found this way," said the men in wonder. "Can we get the

How Pioneers Lived in Covered Wagons

1. The wagons were strong and well-made. The ends of the wagons were higher than the middle so that no babies or bundles could fall out. Chests, boxes, chairs, and tables were loaded inside.

2. At night, the wagons stopped in a great circle. Fires were lit and suppers were cooked. Some people slept in the wagons, while others put up tents. Men guarded the camp at night.

3. In the morning, the train was off by sunrise. It stretched far across the prairie. Oxen pulled most of the wagons, and herds of cows were driven behind.

4. When a river was crossed, a shallow place was found. It is called a ford. Into the water the oxen splashed. Down bumped the wagons. Sometimes the wagons had to be pulled across.

5. If the river was too deep to ford, the cracks in the wagon box were filled up, and the wagon was used for a boat. The animals swam across.

6. Sometimes the wagons had to be dragged up steep trails. At other times, they had to be let down steep cliffs. The men tied ropes to them and let them down slowly.

7. Sometimes Indians attacked. They stole horses, cows, and oxen and burned the wagons. At other times, Indians were friendly. They helped the pioneers by leading them to safety.

8. Day after day, the wagon train went on. Babies and old people rode inside. The rest of the family took turns walking and driving the animals. Some men rode horses.

Questions

1. Why were pioneers fearful of losing the trail going west?

2. If the pioneers came to a river that was shallow enough to wade across, what did they do? If the river was too deep to wade across, what did they do?

3. As people crossed the desert, why did they sometimes need to throw things away? What sort of things did they leave behind?

4. Tell how camp was made at night.

5. Do you think that the covered wagons were made for hard use?

6. What type of animal often pulled the big wagons?

Things to Do

1. Draw a picture of a covered wagon, and color it blue and red.

2. Find out all you can about buffaloes. Look up the word *buffalo* in an encyclopedia or on the Internet. Draw a buffalo mask on a brown paper bag, then cut it out.

3. Draw a picture of mountains. Show where you would go to find a trail between the peaks. The easiest way to get through the mountains is called a mountain pass.

4. Make a list of the animals that went west with the pioneers.

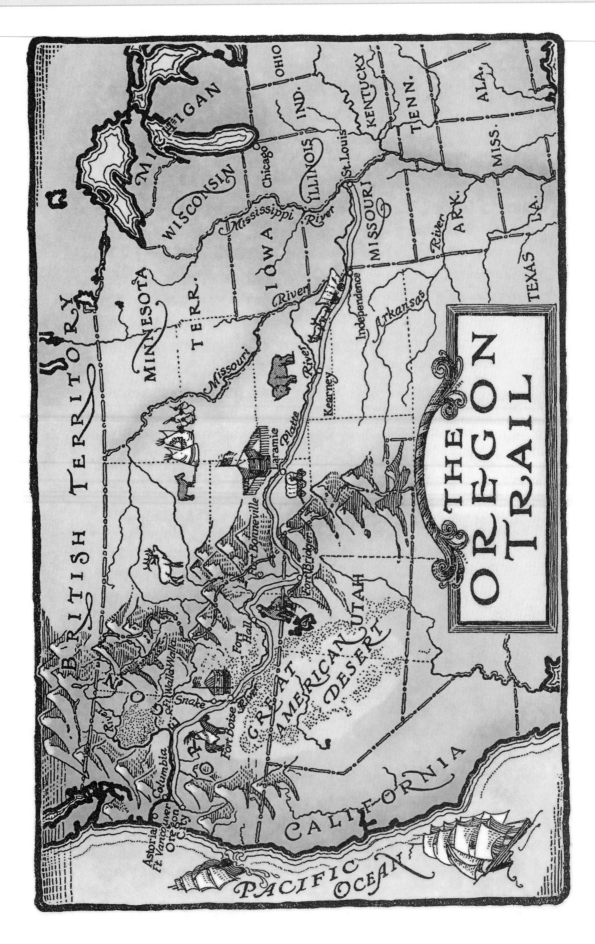

Three Trails through the Mountains

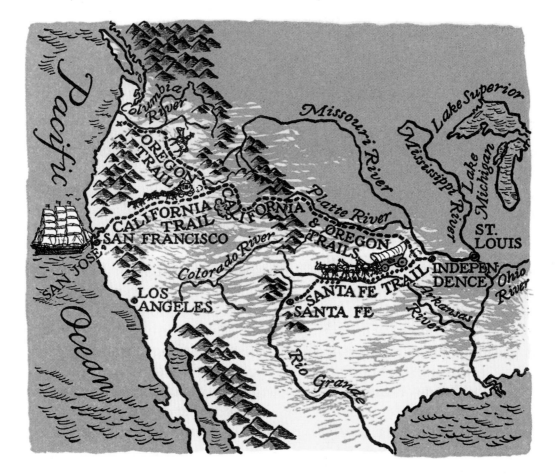

Stories about the Santa Fe Trail, the Oregon Trail,
and the California Trail

In the spring, the little town of Independence, Missouri, was a busy place. At this time, the wagon trains started out from Independence on the long trails west.

Sometimes, a thousand pioneers would be camped outside the little town, waiting. They needed to wait until the snow was off the mountain trails. Then they must start quickly, for they needed to be through the mountains before snow fell again.

Nearly every other shed in Independence was a blacksmith's shop. Clang, clang went hammers on red-hot iron. The wagons must be ready for the long hard trip. The iron rims must be tight. Chains must be ready. Bolts and nails must be made. Burning sparks flew into the air.

The pioneers needed to buy many things to prepare for the long journey. People who were blessed with enough money to spare bought last-minute things for the trip.

"I may need another bag of flour and some coffee," cried one woman.

"I want sugar and salt pork," said another.

The men sold or traded horses and mules and oxen while they waited.

At last, word came that the trail was safe. Off the wagon trains moved. After that, the little town of Independence settled down and became quiet again.

There were three trails that went from the town of Independence. They led to very different parts of North America.

One was the Santa Fe Trail. It went southwest over the Great Plains, across Raton Pass, and along the Rio Grande to the old city of Santa Fe. It is the second oldest city in the United States. Spanish pioneers had built Santa Fe in 1610—ten years before the Pilgrims came to America!

Another was the Oregon Trail. It started out west along the Platte River, crossed South Pass, and then followed the Snake River northwest. After that, the trail led north through the mountains, then it moved west along the roaring Columbia River. Along part of this trail, tall dark trees covered the sides of the mountains.

The third trail was the California Trail. It started out west along the Oregon Trail. Then these trails split on the west side of the Rocky Mountains. After that, the California Trail followed the Humbolt River to Sacramento and the Pacific Ocean.

The next three stories will tell you what the pioneers found at the end of each of these three trails.

Chapter 28
Nick's Sombrero

AT THE END OF
THE SANTA FE TRAIL

Mules are best in dry, rocky terrain. Nick felt sure of it. They are stronger than horses and faster than oxen.

But mules can be mean and hard to manage. Nick had to watch their heels. They were tricky. Still, mules were best.

Nick sat by his father, who was driving three pairs of black mules. The animals trotted quickly along over the dry, rough earth. There was excitement in the air.

The city of Santa Fe was near!

Six weeks before, Nick and his father had left Independence. They had traveled across the plains, where the days were hot and muggy. Then they had crossed over moun-tains, where they nearly froze at night. After that, they had passed through valleys, where the sun beat down, and where there was no water for sixty miles. Day and night, they had kept a sharp watch for Indians. Now that was all over.

Santa Fe was near!

All the men were dressed up in their best clothes. Fine suits and shiny boots had been pulled out of dusty wagons. Nick had changed his torn overalls and faded blue shirt for fresh ones. Santa Fe was near!

The mountains rose blue and soft across the barren valley. Big jackrabbits dashed out from behind bushes. Wolves and coyotes sneaked past.

"Watch out there!" cried Nick.

A big rattlesnake lay on the trail. It was ready to strike. The mules jumped to one side. Then the heavy wheels of the wagon passed over the snake.

The wagon was full of goods to trade. There were bright silks and cotton cloth. There were tools and knives to trade for leather, furs, and silver. This was the first time that Nick had come with his father. This year, Nick, too, was riding into Santa Fe.

There was one thing, however, that bothered Nick. He had no hat. His hair stood up straight on top of his head.

Nick had lost his hat in a storm. One night, thunder had roared. Lightning had flashed. Rain had poured down. Then came a wild wind. Nick had tried to hang on to the little tent where he was sleeping. The wind had blown both him and the tent away.

In God's mercy, it had thrown them against the wheel of a wagon. Nick had hung onto the wheel till the storm passed, but his hat was gone.

"Probably blown clear back to the Missouri River," said one of the men.

It was hard not to have a hat. A hat could be used to dip water from a spring. A hat was useful to fan away the clouds of flies and mosquitoes. At night, you could put it over your face to keep off the mosquitoes. Yes, hats were useful.

The sun was hot. Nick tied a red handkerchief over his head. He sighed. And now, he had to ride into Santa Fe with no hat! He had no hat to wave.

The last night in camp, the men had cut each other's hair. They had trimmed each other's whiskers. They had pulled out their best suits. They had brushed their hats. Today, everyone wore a hat except Nick.

"There's Santa Fe ahead!" shouted his father.

Far ahead, Nick could see fields and trees and houses with flat roofs. A tall church rose among them.

Shouts and cheers came from the men. Guns were fired into the air. Hats were waved. On went the mules at a gallop. Down the last hill came the wagons at top speed.

Around the square in the middle of the town they went. Then they stopped at the old inn at the end of the trail.

"Well, my boy, we've made it!" cried Nick's father.

Nick had never seen a town like Santa Fe. The houses back in Independence were made of wood. But, in Santa Fe, they were made of clay and stone.

People came crowding around the wagons. The women wore full skirts of big colors. They had high combs in their black hair. They wore bright flowers. They spoke Spanish. Nick could not understand what they said.

The men were in white. Some wore red sashes. They had on big wide hats. Nick looked at those hats. Oh, how he wanted one!

"Those big hats are called sombreros," said his father. "How would you like to ride back into Independence with a sombrero on your head?"

There was no more time to think of hats just then. The wagons must be unloaded.

That night, the old inn was alive with laughter and sound. There was dancing, too. Nick and his father watched, as pretty Spanish girls whirled round and round. Then the men threw down their sombreros, and the girls danced lightly around them.

You needed a hat in Santa Fe, even to dance! Nick still had no hat. Sadly, he went back to the wagon. He climbed inside and went to sleep.

The next morning, Nick started out early. He was going to get a hat! He did not know where. And he did not know how, because he had no money. But somehow he was going to get a hat.

His light hair stood on end. His blue eyes were firm. His mind was made up. He was going to get a hat! People smiled as he went by.

At the trader's, there were only big hats.

"How much?" asked Nick. He pointed to a hat.

"Too much and too big," laughed the trader.

Nick put the hat on his head. It covered him—nose, and all. The men in the room began to laugh. Embarrassed, Nick pulled the hat off. He did not like to be laughed at by strangers.

Nick walked across the square. A boy just his age was leaning against the wall. He had on a hat—a wide black hat. True, it was faded. And there was a hole in it, but it was still a good hat.

Nick stopped and looked at it. It was just his size. He took the red handkerchief out of his pocket. He took a knife with a broken point. Then he found a little pocket mirror.

He held them all out toward the boy. He pointed at the hat.

The boy looked surprised. He took off his hat and looked at it. He was fond of that hat. He put the hat on again. He would not trade it.

Nick flashed sunlight with the mirror. He flashed light in the eyes of a mule that stood near. The animal made a loud noise and put its lips back to bite. Nick and the boy laughed. But when Nick pointed to the hat, the boy shook his head.

There was one last thing deep in Nick's pocket. It was the most precious thing that he owned. It was his mouth organ. He could play "Home, Sweet Home," and "Yankee Doodle."

Could Nick bear to offer his mouth organ? Would the boy trade his hat for it?

Slowly and sadly, Nick put the mouth organ to his lips. He started to play "Yankee Doodle."

He played loud and clear. This might be the last tune he was ever to play on his mouth organ. He would do his best.

The boy jumped up. His black eyes shone. He pulled the hat from his head. He held it out to Nick. He pointed to the mouth organ. He wanted it and he wanted it right away!

But Nick would not stop playing. He played through to the end of the tune. Then slowly, he started to hold out the mouth organ toward the boy.

Suddenly, there was a sound behind him. Someone cried, "Bravo!" Something was clapped on Nick's head. Nick turned quickly. There stood his father.

"I've been hunting all over town for you," said his father. "Never would have found you if it hadn't been for that music."

Back into Nick's pocket dropped the mouth organ.

His hands went to his head.

"How's that for a fit?" laughed his father.

Nick felt something large and round and smooth. It was a hat. It was a sombrero. It was just the right size for him.

The boy watched sadly. The mouth organ was safe in Nick's pocket. The boy put his old hat back on his head. He leaned back against the wall. Oh well, some day he'd have a mouth organ, too.

Nick waved good-bye. Then out came the organ. As he followed his father, Nick played for the entire world to hear.

> Yankee Doodle came to town
> Riding on a pony,
> Stuck a feather in his hat
> And called it Macaroni!

When Nick finished the tune, he took his hat from his head to look at it. His smile was as big and wide as the hat. He had a real sombrero.

"Everybody in Independence will know I've been to Santa Fe," he said proudly. ❏

Chapter 29
The Twins and Nell

AT THE END OF THE OREGON TRAIL

Jed Johnson was the first pioneer to go up the valley so far. He had built his cabin at the edge of the forest. Behind it rose huge fir trees. It seemed to his little sister Nell as though the sky rested on the trees.

As Jed was working hard in the fields, Nell brought the twins out to see their father. The twins were one and a half years old. They were very young pioneers. They had just learned to walk. Nell had a rope around her waist. Bobby was tied to one end, and Davy was tied to the other.

Sadly, trouble had come to the little cabin under the fir trees. Life in a pioneer cabin was hard. Mary, Jed's wife, lay ill.

"I've got to get Mary to a doctor," Jed said. "It's eight miles down the trail to the nearest town."

Ten-year-old Nell nodded. She looked very serious, as she dug the toe of her shoe into the soft earth.

"You'll have to stay alone with the twins," said Jed.

Up till now, there were no neighbors to turn to for help. Also, Jed had only one horse for traveling. He had lost his ox team on the way out west. So Jed had to drive a horse and a cow together for the plowing.

"I can hold Mary on the horse and walk beside her," said Jed. "But with only one horse, I can't take the twins and you along."

"Don't you worry," said Nell. "I will manage."

The cows were tied near the house where they could graze. Jed left the sheep and pigs in the barn. With bears and wolves around, the barn was almost like a fort. So Jed barred the door to protect the animals.

Mary looked white and weak as Jed lifted her up on the horse. Jed would let her stop often and rest on a buffalo robe under a tree. Nell ran out with food for them to carry on the trip.

"There's a pistol on the shelf. It's loaded," said Jed softly. "A gun's too heavy for you."

Nell nodded. Pioneer women and girls, as well as men, needed to learn to handle guns. So Jed had taught Nell to aim the big pistol and to fire.

Nell and the twins waved good-bye. They watched the horse disappear down the trail. Then they turned back and went into the little, one-room cabin.

There was plenty for Nell to do. First, she tied the rope that held the twins to a peg. Then she ran out for more wood.

"Milk!" demanded Davy as she came back.

She filled a tin cup for him. He tipped it up. Nothing could be seen but his golden curls above the cup. Indian women loved to pat those curls. When they saw the twins, they smiled and reached out their hands to touch the boys' hair.

Nell turned toward the fire. But the next second, there came a loud wail from

Bobby. Davy was pouring his milk over Bobby. Then he beat Bobby on the head with the cup.

"Davy, stop it, you naughty boy!" cried Nell, as she snatched the cup away.

But Bobby had stopped crying. He thought it was funny to have milk running off his nose.

"I'll take you two rascals out of doors," Nell said.

Two big spoons, some stones, and an iron kettle kept the twins busy for an hour. Nell sat with her knitting. Then Bobby wanted Davy's spoon. They both began to cry. Nell ran in for some food. It was time for dinner.

Nell sat on the step with a big bowl of soup. A twin sat on either side of her. First she fed one, and then the other. They opened their

mouths like little birds.

After dinner, Nell tried to get the twins to take naps. But they were very wide-awake. They laughed and rolled over on the bed. Then Bobby fell off one side of the bed, and Davy fell off the other.

At last, Nell thought of something her grandmother had told her to do. Grandmother had said, "When you are at your wit's end with a baby, remember to try molasses. It will help you out."

Nell took a little molasses from the jug. She rubbed it on the babies' fat fingers. Then she pulled two little feathers from the feather bed. She gave each baby a feather. The feathers stuck to their fingers. The babies tried to pick them off with one hand but they only stuck to the other.

The twins stopped crying. This was a new game! They began to laugh and shout. But at last, they grew sleepy. Eyes began to close. Nell did not mean to drop asleep too, but she was very tired. The smell of the fir trees came in the window. Only the buzz of a fly could be heard. Soon all was quiet in the little house.

Nell slept soundly. Then, suddenly, she awoke. She heard strange noises outside. For a moment she lay still. Then she jumped up. Oh, she should not have slept! What was happening? Something terrible?

The cows were mooing loudly. Then a

rope broke and she heard the sound of running hoofs. Nell started toward the door. Then she stopped. She stood as still as though she had been turned to stone.

A huge black head was looking in at the door!

There came a low growl. It was a big black bear! Slowly it rose up on its hind legs and looked about.

It seemed bigger than the whole house. The bear filled the whole doorway, but it did not come inside. Nell watched with horror.

Bears love sweets. This one had smelled the molasses. It reached out a huge paw. It reached for the molasses jug that Nell had left on the table close by the door. Nell could see sharp claws on the bear's paw. Those claws could tear off the hair from a man's head. One stroke from those great paws could crush a man.

Down tumbled the jug from the table. The molasses spilled and ran out the door and down the step. The bear dropped on all fours. Out came a long pink tongue. It began to lick up the

delicious brown stream. Then it followed the molasses out the door. Never had the big bear tasted anything so good.

Nell jumped forward. She snatched up the jug and threw it outside. It broke into a dozen pieces. She slammed the heavy door shut and barred it tightly. Suddenly, there was a surprised and angry growl from outside. A big paw scratched at the door. But then, the bear found the rest of the molasses and began to lick it up.

As Nell turned away from the door, she saw two small faces watching her from the bed. She saw four large blue eyes. Oh dear, she thought, now they will be frightened and begin to cry.

But all Davy said was "Bow-wow!" in a sweet voice.

All that Bobby said was, "Bow-wow, all gone!"

Nell started to laugh and cry at the same time. She ran to the bed and hugged the twins.

What should she do next? She heard excited sounds from the barn. The animals smelled danger and were afraid. For a moment Nell thought she heard the sound of a horse coming. Perhaps Jed was back! But Jed was many miles away.

"I have got to get rid of the beast!" thought Nell.

She looked at the pistol on the shelf. She was afraid of the big, heavy thing. But she took it down carefully. Then she climbed

to tell him everything at once. A bear had come. The cows had run off. She had wounded the bear, but not killed it. The twins were safe and asleep. "How was Mary?" she asked, nearly out of breath.

Jed threw his strong arms around Nell and held her close. He told her that Mary was comfortable. All she needed was rest and nursing. He was proud of Nell. She must not worry about the cows.

"I'll follow that bear's trail in the morning," said Jed. "We'll have a fine big bearskin to lay in front of the fire. It will be a warm place for the twins to play in winter."

onto a stool by the window. The bear was still outside, licking the broken jug. It was so near she could almost touch it!

Nell held the heavy pistol as steady as she could. She counted three and then fired. There came a loud, angry howl from outside. But Nell could not see what had happened. As the heavy pistol went off, her stool tipped over. Down she went, "Crash!" When she got to her feet, there was no sign of the bear. But a trail of blood led off toward the woods.

It was late that night when Jed came home. The forest was as black as a pocket. He could not see the trail. But the tired horse knew the way.

Nell ran out to meet him. She tried

Just then, Nell heard a sound of trampling in the woods. She gripped Jed's arm. He raised his gun. Then he gave a laugh. A white face peered through the

bushes. They could barely see it in the starlight. It was one of the cows! Soon the other one followed. They had come back to be milked.

Nell clapped her hands for joy. Then she ran for the milk pails. ❏

Chapter 30
The Great News

AT THE END OF THE CALIFORNIA TRAIL

It was still dark. Fog blew in from the Pacific Ocean. Ken sat all alone on his small trunk. He was waiting for the stagecoach. He felt in his pocket for his money. Was it safe? Was it there? Yes, it was there.

His mother's name was on his trunk. It was put on in brass tacks. But she seemed very far away. She was back in Iowa with the younger children. And Ken felt very much alone.

There was one big question in Ken's mind. Would his father meet him? Would he find his father?

Ken had come west with neighbors. He had helped care for their cattle. For nearly two thousand miles he had walked. Day after day after day, he had walked, following the long line of wagons. Now, at

last, he was in San Francisco.

His friends had left him before the sun was up. They were going north, but he was going south.

"You wait here till the stagecoach comes," they had said. "Good-bye and God-speed."

"Thanks. God be with you, too," called Ken. He had felt very much alone as the wagons moved off into the fog.

Ken's father had come to California the year before. It seemed as though everybody in the world was rushing to California in the year 1849. Gold had been found in California!

But Ken's father had found little of the precious metal. He had nearly broken his back working up in the mountains. Then he had gone to the town of San Jose, where he had started a store. He had done well. So he had written for Ken to come out to help him. Ken was to come the first chance he had.

So here sat Ken in the fog, waiting for

the stagecoach. Would his father meet him? Would he find his father? His mother had written that he had started, but it took months for letters to get to California in those days.

The fog began to lift. Round and red, the sun rose from behind the mountains. Ken walked up and down the road to get warm. Then, suddenly, he stopped.

He looked down on a lovely sight. The water was full of ships. People were coming to California by water as well as by land.

As Ken watched, another ship came sailing in. She was larger than the rest and had

I wait?" cried a woman. She had three children and a big pile of boxes and a trunk.

"This way, ma'am," shouted one man. "Have your trunk weighed."

"What? Fifteen dollars to take that trunk?" cried the woman.

"Leave it in the middle of the road, if you'd rather," said the man.

There was nothing to do but pay. Just then the first stagecoach drove in. The woman hurried her children aboard.

Ken watched anxiously for the coach for San Jose. Soon it came. It was a fine sight, with six black horses. They were eager to

great white sails. She was a clipper ship. In she came, through the opening that led in from the Pacific Ocean beyond. The opening is now called the Golden Gate.

Ken gave a jump. Where was he? Was his trunk safe? Was it time for the stagecoach to start? He ran back to his place. A few people were already there, and more were coming.

Now that the sun was up, the town awoke. People hurried here and there. Several coaches were to start off in different directions.

Men hurried through the crowd. "This way, sir," they shouted. "Here you are, ma'am. Your stage will start from over there."

"Where will my stage be? Where should

be off. Men held the heads of the lead horses.

"Up you go if you have the fare, son," shouted a big man with a red face.

Ken counted out his money. He had just enough for himself and his trunk. He climbed to a seat on top of the coach. A woman with a wide skirt and a big hatbox sat next him. Her skirt nearly covered him up.

"Just think!" she said to Ken. "We're going sixty miles in six hours. I hope we don't have an accident. My sister was in a stagecoach that went rolling over a cliff—people, horses, and all together. It was dreadful."

"No accidents on this line," called the driver. "This line has Concord coaches. None better made. This coach, here, came all the way from Concord, New Hampshire, way back East."

"How did it get over the mountains?" asked Ken. "Came round South America by boat," said the driver.

There was no more talk. Just then came shouting and cheering. Something exciting had happened. Ken jumped up in his place to see. Men were throwing their hats into the air. Guns were being fired.

Great news had just reached San Francisco. California had been made a state!

Another star had been added to the flag of the United States of America. It was a star for the new state of California. It was the thirty-first star, for the United States had been growing since Washington's day. Now there were thirty-one states instead of thirteen.

"California has been made a state!" everyone shouted.

Ken nearly fell off his seat, but the woman next to him kept a hold on his coat.

Then a man in a wide hat came pushing through the crowd. He was the Governor. He was to carry the news to the people in San Jose. The Governor climbed onto the coach where Ken sat.

A horn blew. The men jumped back from the horses' heads. Off the horses galloped.

Ken held his breath. It seemed like flying. He had never ridden so fast before. The coach was hung on heavy leather straps. It rocked to and fro.

Then Ken saw, through the dust, that there was another coach beside them. There were two stagecoaches going to San Jose. Which would get there first? Which would carry the news?

Off across the bare, flat ground the horses galloped. The drivers did not care to keep on a road. Off toward the brown hills, the two coaches raced.

People along the way ran out to see why the stagecoaches were going so fast.

"California is a state!" everyone shouted.

The horses' sides were covered with foam. They were panting, and they were tired. But a race is a race. Neither coach would let the other coach get ahead.

At last, a low brick building came in sight. Fresh horses waited there. The horses made a last plunge. The coach on which Ken rode rattled up to the building. By this time, his coach was well ahead.

It did not take very long to change the horses. Fresh ones were ready. Away they galloped. Ken's coach was still in the lead.

The way grew rougher. Suddenly there came a terrible bump. Ken flew into the air. He came down on the hatbox of the lady next to him. People screamed. The coach stopped.

A wheel was caught in a hole. The horses strained and pulled. They could not get it out. So men jumped down to help the horses. But while they worked, the other coach went thundering past. It was an awful moment. Ken was so excited about winning the race that he wanted to howl with rage.

Just then the men and horses got the wheel free. In another moment they were tearing along. Little by little, they gained on the other coach.

"We've got to win!" shouted Ken. "We've got to win! The Governor's aboard!"

"We're going to win!" said the driver. He knew his horses. He urged them on.

Never was there such a ride. The horses galloped neck to neck. The people were nearly shaken to pieces. Ken shouted so much that he could hardly speak.

It was two o'clock when the stages dashed into San Jose. The coach on which Ken rode was just ahead. His coach had won the race! The horses were pulled to a halt, and the coaches stopped.

"California is a state! " shouted the driver.

People came running from every side. They cheered and clapped. People began climbing down from the stagecoach. Suddenly, Ken felt very much alone.

He could see no one he knew. In all the excitement, he had forgotten that he was all alone. Would his father meet him? Would he find his father? What should he do if no one met him? Perhaps his mother's letter had not arrived.

For a few moments Ken stood by his small trunk and looked around.

"Waiting for someone?" asked a man.

"I'm looking for my father," said Ken.

"California is a pretty big place to lose your father in," said the man.

Just then Ken saw a tall man coming toward him. He had a wide hat and a long black beard. He also wore a pistol at his belt. Ken looked at him carefully. Then he gave a cry of surprise.

The tall man was coming straight toward him. It was his father. Ken had not known him with a beard. It was nearly two years since he had seen his father.

The next minute Ken was given a big hug and swung off his feet. In all the excitement, he did not forget to tell the news.

"California is a state!" cried Ken. "And we brought the Governor, and our stagecoach won the race. And here I am!

"Ready to grow up with the country," laughed his father. "I'm glad you're here at last. I've been meeting stagecoaches ever since your mother's letter came."

Ken's father picked up the trunk and carried it on his shoulder.

"It's good to see your mother's old trunk," he said. "I hope she and the children will be coming out next year."

Ken followed his father through the little town. It had been a Spanish town once. Now it was filled with pioneers from many lands. The bells still hung in the old church that Spanish priests had built for the Indians. The bells rang out to welcome Ken to his new home. ❑

How the Blacksmith Worked

1. Big bellows blew air on the fire and made it blaze. The place where the fire burned was called the forge. The blacksmith wore a heavy leather apron.

2. The blacksmith held a piece of iron in the fire. He held it in a pair of tongs. The iron became red hot. Then it became so hot that it turned white.

3. The iron became soft because it was so very hot. Then the blacksmith hammered it on his anvil. Sparks flew everywhere from the hot iron.

4. The blacksmith made many things that the pioneers used. He made plows, shovels, and axes. He mended wagon wheels and chains.

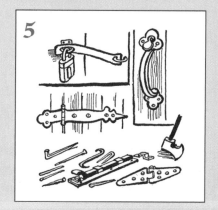

5. In his spare time, the blacksmith made nails. Each nail had to be made by hand. He made hinges for doors and latches to hold them shut.

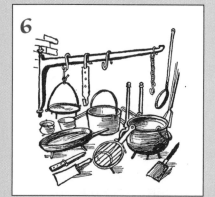

6. He made iron kettles and pots. He made the cranes and the pothooks to hold the kettles over the fire. He also made iron spoons and knives and forks.

7. When a horse needed a new shoe, the blacksmith pounded the iron into a horseshoe. Then he cooled it in a tub of water.

8. He cut away some of the horse's hoof and fitted the shoe. Then he nailed it on with nails he had made himself.

Unit 10 Review

Questions

1. Why was Independence, Missouri, such a busy place during pioneer days?

2. What types of things did the blacksmith make?

3. What are the names of the oceans that lay east and west of the United States?

4. These stories tell about three trails west. What were the three trails called?

5. Why were the stagecoaches racing to reach the city of San Jose?

6. Which city in Missouri was started by the French people?

Things to Do

1. Do a map study for this unit. Find the following places on a map:

Great Plains	*Rio Grande*	*Santa Fe*	*Rocky Mountains*
Platte River	*Snake River*	*Oregon*	*Columbia River*
Sacramento	*San Fancisco*	*California*	*Pacific Ocean*

   There is a state and a river named Missouri. Find both on a map. Where is Independence, Missouri, found on the map?

2. Visit a blacksmith shop if there is one near you. If not, ask your grandfather or some older man you know if he saw a blacksmith shop when he was a boy.

3. Make a list of the devices and tools that you would find in a blacksmith shop.

4. Make your own sombrero out of poster board and felt. Have your teacher help you.

   Draw a big circle on a poster board, about one and a half feet across. Then, inside the larger circle, draw a smaller circle the size of your head. Cut out the smaller circle. Then cut away the poster board around the outside of the larger circle. Now you have a big ring.

   Next, cut out a circle of felt, about two feet across. You will now glue the felt on the ring of poster board. First, put glue around the inside and outside edges of the ring of the poster board. Then, evenly press the edge of the felt circle all around the outside edge of the ring. Next, press the felt evenly on the inside edge of the ring. Now you have a sombrero.

5. Purchase a hand organ or harmonica, and learn how to play the song "Yankee Doodle."

TRAILS USED BY EMIGRANTS TO WESTWARD LANDS ABOUT 1850

Home on the Plains

A Story of Pioneers from Norway

Pioneers had rushed to California to try to find gold. Many stayed and built homes along the Pacific Ocean. There were many cities and towns and farms all the way from the Atlantic Ocean to beyond the Mississippi River. Yet, in the middle part of our country, Indians still lived on the Great Plains.

Then, little by little, the last pioneers began moving onto the Great Plains. Little by little, they took the last of the Indians' land.

Indian chiefs called their young warriors together. They tried to keep their land. A hundred battles were fought. Many pioneers and many Indians were killed.

Some of the Indians were paid a little for their land, but money did not make up for lost homes and lost hunting grounds. A little land was still left to them, but it was often poor land.

As the years went by, more and more people came to this country to live. In 1862, a law was passed that gave free farmland to anyone who would go west and live on it. More and more pioneers hurried west.

Some of these pioneers came from the country of Norway, which is in Europe. Norway is a country by the sea. In Norway, steep cliffs drop down to the water. Deep forests cover much of the land.

The Great Plains was very different from the land that these pioneers had left. Often there was not one tree in sight on the Great Plains. Mile after mile of grassy land stretched away. The winds howled in winter. The hot sun beat down in summer. Pioneers from Norway found this new land very strange.

There were so few trees that it was hard to build houses. These pioneers had to build their first houses out of sod. They cut squares of sod and piled them on top of each other.

Little by little, sod houses took the place of Indian tepees. Children from Norway now played where Indians had once sat by campfires and watched the war dance. And men plowed the ground where buffaloes had grazed.

What was it like, coming from Norway to build a sod home on this great, lonely plain? The next story will tell you.

The Sod House

Chapter 31
Breaking Earth

A sod house! That was a strange thing. A lump came in Hilda's throat. She did not want to live in a sod house.

The two older boys, Olaf and Eric, did not care what kind of house they lived in. It was this fine rich land that pleased them. It was wonderful land to plow and to plant. It was as flat as your hand. It had cost them nothing!

"Come on, boys," shouted Father. "Fasten the oxen to the plow. We'll break the earth."

Hilda looked around. She looked out over the big, lonely, empty land. She had never thought that there could be such a land.

The boys lifted a plow from one of the wagons that had brought them to this place. They fastened two of the oxen to the plow.

"Here we go!" shouted Father.

Father held the plow firmly. He pressed it into the earth, as the boys led the oxen. Off they started. Slowly the plow cut a deep, long black line into the earth. The boys cheered. It was an exciting moment.

"It's fine rich earth," said Mother.

Back and forth went the plow, turning up the sod. While the oxen rested, the boys cut the sod into squares. They left the squares to dry in the sun. They would use them to make a house.

But Hilda did not want to live in a sod house. She thought of Grandmother's neat house back in Norway. There were big curtains at the windows and big feather beds to sleep in. On summer days, salt breezes from the ocean blew in. How Hilda wished that she could run down to the shore now to watch the fishing boats!

"We can let the sod house wait till cold

weather," said Father. "We can live in the tent for a while." He wanted to get the fields plowed.

Mother pleaded, "Can't the fields wait? We need a house for the children."

Father prayed about what to do first, and

he decided to start building the house at once. Each day the sod walls grew higher.

"You can't use sod for a roof," said Hilda. "What will we have for a roof?"

"This house isn't going to have any roof," teased Olaf.

"Snow will keep you warm in winter," joked Eric.

"Go, get your work done," said Mother. "Of course there's going to be a roof, Hilda. Father will have to get logs to hold it."

Father hated to stop work to go for the logs. But the boys thought that a trip would be fun. Some trees grew near a river, several miles away. After the logs were cut, the boys could go for a swim.

The next day, Father and the boys started off. Hilda stayed and helped her mother

wash clothes at the spring nearby. There was bread to bake, too, in an open iron oven by the campfire. Then Hilda and her mother sat down to patch the boys' shirts.

The day grew very hot. It was like an oven inside the tent. Suddenly, Hilda could stand it no longer.

"I hate it here!" she sobbed. "I want to go back home."

Mother stroked Hilda's hair. "There, dear," she said softly. "You're homesick. It's best to cry it out."

"Why did we have to come?" cried Hilda.

"It's this fine land your father wants," said her mother. "It was a hard life in Norway for your father, fishing in the winter storms."

"Can't we go back?" asked Hilda.

"It would break your father's heart," said her mother. "Come, shut your eyes and take a nap. I'll tell you a story about when I was a little girl."

She told about the day in Norway when the cows were driven way up on the mountains to graze. She had gone along and had lost her way. The women had called, and the men had hunted. There was such a great fuss! Then at last, she had been found. She was curled up beside a big cow, which was lying down chewing its cud. There she was, lying fast asleep.

On went Mother's voice until Hilda, too, was asleep. Mother sat looking at her. It was a hard country for a little girl. The boys were all right. One minute they were chasing prairie dogs. The next minute they were begging their father to let them shoot ducks with the gun. They were up to plenty of mischief, those boys. But it was harder for a girl. ❏

Chapter 32
Winter

Snow came early that year. The sod hut was done in time. There was only one room and a shed for the oxen, but it was done.

The air was so full of snowflakes that Hilda could not see out of either little window. Much good it did to have windows! The house was dark and dreary.

It was good that Father and the boys had spent two weeks cutting wood for the fire. The little iron stove was kept red hot. But the sod walls of the house and the dirt floor were damp and cold.

Father and Eric had made a trip to the nearest town. They had bought flour, bacon, beans, coffee, and sugar. There was enough to eat in the little sod house, but there was little fun. The one room was too

crowded. Olaf and Eric began to quarrel. Then Eric started to teased Hilda.

"School!" said Mother firmly. "What you three need is school."

She took out a Bible and a spelling book from the big chest that had come with them. Father split slabs of wood to write on. Charcoal could be used for pencils.

Hilda wanted to draw pictures of the sea and rocks and boats. But Mother said, "No drawing, till lessons are learned."

In the evenings, they sang. Mother had a sweet voice. The children learned all the hymns of the faith and the old, Norwegian songs.

It was only December. There were January, February, and March still ahead. It seemed to Hilda as though the snow would never stop. Oh, how she longed for other girls to play with!

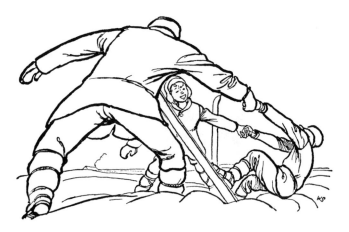

Some of the days were fair. The sun shone so brightly then that the light on the snow was blinding. The boys made skis. Once, Olaf fell into a snowbank. His two skis waved in the air. Eric and his father had to come and pull him out.

At last January and February passed. As March came, Mother began to watch the food with care. The flour was low. The bacon was almost gone.

"How soon can you make a trip to town?" asked Mother.

The sugar and coffee gave out, but still Father said, "Not quite yet."

Then one sunny morning he said, "The snow's nearly gone. We'll start today. We'll be back the day after tomorrow."

Eric had gone to town in the fall. It was Olaf's turn now.

"Will Mother and I never go to town?" thought Hilda selfishly. "It's always the boys and Father who go."

Hilda watched the wagon move off across the wide plain. The land was so flat that she could see the wagon for nearly an hour. It grew smaller and smaller. Then it disappeared. Tears came to Hilda's eyes.

For two days, the warm spring breeze blew. Then, on the third day, the wind changed. Clouds raced across the sky. The air filled with snow.

That night, there was no sleep in the sod house. Eric kept the stove red hot, and Mother kept food warm. Everyone was

thinking of the biting wind and the snow. And they all were worried about the ox team struggling through the storm.

There came a sound at the door. Mother jumped to her feet, but it was only the wind.

Eric could sit still no longer. "Let me take my skis and go out to meet Father and Olaf," he begged.

"You have no way of finding them in the storm," said his mother.

A noise came again. Eric ran to the door. Then the others followed him. This time it must be something besides the wind. Suddenly the door swung open. In came the icy wind. In came, also, a tall white snowman. He had something in his arms. It was Father carrying Olaf!

"Get the oxen under cover as fast as you can, Eric," shouted Father. "See that they get extra food." Eric obeyed at once.

Olaf lay on the bed. Mother and Hilda rubbed his face and feet with snow to bring the blood back into them. Father walked back and forth swinging his arms and stamping. He drank a big bowl of hot soup.

At last, Olaf opened his eyes. He was warm, and he was sleepy, so sleepy. When Father saw that Olaf was all right, he threw himself down beside the boy. The two slept as though they would never wake again.

The next morning, Father and Olaf told of the trip. They had reached the town safely. They had bought all they needed and started for home. They were only ten miles from home when the snow came. They could not tell which way to go. No tracks showed through the snow.

They had wandered about in the snow and wind for eight hours. But at last, the oxen had found the way. At the end of the day, the patient beasts had found their way home.

Hilda sat and listened. She thought, "This was a terrible land of cold and storms." In summer, the sun was a ball of fire, and the days were hot. In winter, the storms blew across the plains. The snow piled up until the houses were nearly covered. Sometimes, people were buried in snow and froze to death within a mile of their own homes. It was a cruel land.

"I have plenty of seed for the fields," said Father. "We'll sow wheat as soon as the snow melts."

"He is thinking only of his fields," thought Hilda bitterly. "He has already forgotten the terrible trip." She could not understand her father's love of the land and of farming.

She gave a sigh. She could not love this strange new land! ❏

Chapter 33
Spring

Spring flowers came at last. Down by the flowing spring, little frogs sang. Now Father and the boys started early and worked late.

Then one day, Eric came racing toward the house. "Someone is coming!" he shouted.

Was it Indians? The Indians had been angry and bitter of late. They often raided the farms of the settlers in this area.

Father got his gun. All of the family quickly climbed onto the roof of the sod house. Then, far off across the prairie, they saw a line of wagons.

"Covered wagons," shouted Olaf.

"It's a whole village," cried Eric.

There were six wagons, a dozen cows, and some horses. Father and the boys ran out to meet them. Hilda followed more slowly. She wondered who these newcomers were.

Mother put the coffee pot on the stove. The travelers must stop. They must come in and eat fresh bread and drink hot coffee.

It was months since Mother had seen other women. So she got out the best she had to serve her guests. Father took the men out at once to look at his fields. Also, Eric

and Olaf found boys their own age. No more work that day!

At first, Hilda stood alone watching. There were no other girls. Then suddenly her face brightened. There were babies being lifted out of the wagons—three babies and a little one who just began to walk. She ran over to them.

"Here, Hilda," said the baby's mother. "Hold this one."

Hilda took a fat roly-poly baby in her arms. The baby began to laugh and coo. Hilda held her tightly.

For the next two days, Hilda forgot how lonely she had been. She played with the babies all day. One of them slept with her at night. And the one who just began to walk followed her everywhere she went.

For two days, the wagon train camped near the sod house. One man had a fiddle. Each evening, he played for everyone to enjoy. Most of all, Hilda liked the dancing.

"Oh?" thought Hilda, "perhaps these people will take up land here near us. Now perhaps we shall have neighbors."

Father showed the men what good land it was. He urged them to stay. There was much talk, but it did no good. The people decided to go farther.

So they were not to have neighbors after all! The boys were very sad. For Hilda, it did not seem as though she could say good-bye to the babies.

But there was nothing to be done about it. Off moved the long line of wagons. But one wagon stayed behind.

Hilda's mother called to her. "I want to talk to you, Hilda," said Mother quietly. "One of these families has decided to turn back. They are going back to Norway. You could go with them."

"Oh, Mother," began Hilda. Her heart beat fast.

"You could go back to live with Grandmother," said Mother.

Hilda looked at her mother. She could hardly believe her ears. Go back to Norway! Have other girls to play with! Have a real house to live in!

Then suddenly Hilda stopped. Could she leave her mother? Next winter, would she be happy in the big warm kitchen at Grandmother's? Would she forget the little sod house on the plains? When she grew up and told stories to her own little girls, how would she feel? The boys would tell their sons of the first years of "breaking earth." She would have to say that she had given up and gone back to Grandmother's.

Hilda threw her arms about her mother. "I'll stay here! I'll never go back!" she cried. "I don't care what happens!"

"Think well, Hilda," said her mother. "Winter will come again. It is a long, hard time."

"I have thought," cried Hilda. "I'm going to stay here with you and Father and my brothers."

Just then there came a cheer. Hilda jumped with surprise. Her father was standing just behind her. He caught her up in his arms and hugged her.

"Good for you, Hilda!" he said. "You are going to stand by us! In a few years, we'll have a better house. You'll see!"

Two heads looked in at the door. Two pairs of blue eyes looked at Hilda. So Olaf and Eric knew, too!

Eric and Olaf wanted to know what she had decided. They wanted her to stay!

"Hilda is not going away!" said their father. "She's going to stay with us."

There were shouts from the two boys. They turned cartwheels and stood on their heads. Hilda laughed in spite of herself. Suddenly she was happy, for the Lord had taught her to be content regardless of her difficulties.

"I'll teach you how to ski this winter," said Eric.

"I'll make you a sled," said Olaf.

"And I have news," said Father. "A man has just ridden by. The other wagons have turned around. They are coming back to take up land here. We shall have neighbors after all."

Hilda jumped up and clapped her hands. The babies were coming back. She was staying with Mother and Father and the boys. Living in a sod house was not going to be so bad after all. ❏

1. Corn was planted in little hills. Four kernels were put in each hill. The Indians had corn before the pioneers came. They taught the pioneers how to plant it.

How the Pioneers Raised Corn and Wheat

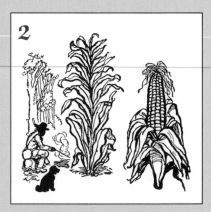

2. Corn was easy to use. As soon as the ears were ripe, they could be roasted and eaten. Or else, the corn could be dried and saved to use later.

3. Corn was often pounded into yellow corn meal in a hollow log. Sometimes a small tree was fastened to the pounder to help lift it up and down.

4. In the fall, the cornstalks were tied into stacks. They looked like Indian tepees. The children played in them and made corncob dolls.

5. Corn would grow in rough ground. Wheat needed well-cleared ground. Stones had to be taken away so that the plow could cut into the earth.

6. Ripe wheat could not be eaten at once. The seeds must be beaten from the stalks. Then the wheat was tossed in the air, and the straw was blown away.

7. The wheat was put between two millstones, which ground it into rich flour. Water from a stream turned the millstone.

8. Corn bread was good. Corn meal kept better than white flour, but people were glad to get white bread and cake.

Questions

1. What are the names of the children in the story "Home on the Plains"?

2. Why was the new home on the plains better for the boys than for Hilda?

3. What were some of the things about Hilda's old home that she longed for in her new home?

4. What was the name of the country from which Hilda had come?

5. What did Hilda's mother find for the children to do during the winter?

6. When Hilda grew up, do you think that she was glad that she had stayed in the sod house?

Things to Do

1. Look back at the stories in this unit. Pick out a scene from one of them to act out. Choose someone to guess the scene you are acting.

2. Which story did you like best in this unit? Tell why you liked it best.

3. Draw a picture of a sod house. Or, with the help of your parents, build a small-scale model of a sod house.

4. Do a map study. Ask your teacher to write down all the names that you can think of that you have read about in this book. Make headings like these:

Places   *Oceans*   *Rivers*   *People*

See if you can find five of the places on a map.

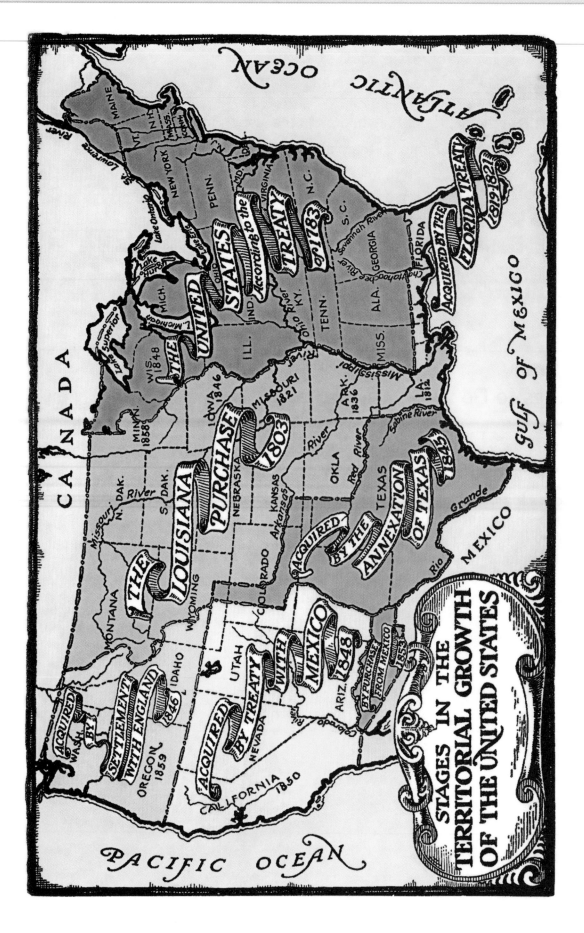

Moving West by Railroad

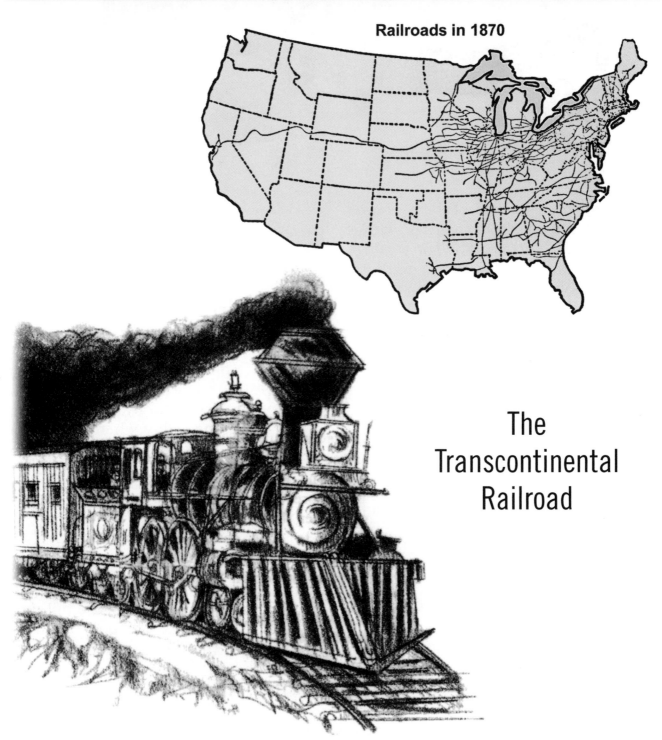

Railroads in 1870

The
Transcontinental
Railroad

The Greatest Pioneer of All

The greatest pioneer of them all was born in a one-room cabin. His father had built it of logs. It had no window, and the floor was dirt. The mother and baby lay on a rough bed with a bearskin thrown over them.

The baby was dressed in a little yellow skirt and a tiny linen shirt. They were made of homespun. He was small and ruddy.

A neighbor's boy came from down the road to look at the new baby.

"He won't amount to much," said the thoughtless boy.

Even so, the little pioneer grew bigger. He had few chances to go to school. He learned to read. He read every book that he could get hold of. He read by the light of the open fire. He learned to write with a bit of charcoal.

When he was eight years old, he could swing an ax. He learned to cut down trees and to split logs into fence rails. His father kept moving west. The baby had been born in Kentucky. Then the family moved to Indiana. After that, they moved to Illinois. Each time they moved, the boy helped his father build a new log cabin.

He grew very tall. He grew very strong. His first long trip away from home was by flatboat down the Mississippi River. Most people said that you could trust him. People often said that he was fair and intelligent.

At last, more and more people came to know this boy who had grown to be a man. More and more people liked to hear him talk. He told funny stories. He made people laugh. He also made people think. He could be serious as well as funny.

At last, came a day when the people of the United States were voting for a new President. There was great excitement and anger in the land, and many disagreed about who should be the nation's leader. Who was to be the next President? Who would be chosen?

The tall and awkward man waited for the news. Who was to be the next President?

At long last, word came. The tall man had been chosen. He was to go to Washington to live in the White House. His name was Abraham Lincoln.

So this pioneer baby, born in a log cabin, grew up and went to the White House. This little boy grew up to become the sixteenth

President of the United States of America.

There had been great changes in our country by the time Abraham Lincoln became President. Slowly our country was changing, from a land of log cabins and homespun cloth to a land where machines and engines were being invented. In those days, men had invented many new things.

During the 1760s, Mr. James Hargreaves invented a machine to spin thread. One person at a machine could spin in a day as much as a thousand women with spinning wheels. Later, Sir Richard Arkwright improved on this invention. In 1793, Mr. Samuel Slater built the first American cotton mill that made a profit.

In 1807, Mr. Fulton invented a steam engine to run a boat.

"A boat run by an engine!" some people cried. "It will blow up. It is not safe." And some of the first engines did blow up.

Steam engines were also invented to pull trains. In 1826, Colonel John Stevens and his sons built the first American steam locomotive. Four years later, his son, Robert L. Stevens, developed the railway T-rail and the railroad spike—both of which are still used today. T-rails, or railroad tracks, were laid on wooden ties for locomotives to run on. At first, cows walked along the tracks and got in the way. Also, sparks from the engines set fire to ladies' hats as they rode on the coaches.

In spite of problems, more machines were invented. Sewing machines were made, so that all the clothes did not have to be sewed by hand. Machines were invented to make nails. Machines were invented to cut wheat and harvest corn.

When young Abe Lincoln moved to Illinois with his father, he went in a big, homemade wagon. But when Abraham Lincoln went to Washington in 1861, he did not go by covered wagon. He did not even go on horseback or in a stagecoach. He went on a train!

It was very different from our trains today. The engine had a tall smokestack. Black smoke streamed from it. But it could go more than twenty miles an hour. It could go farther in one hour than a covered wagon could go in a day.

More and more miles of railroad track were being laid each year. By 1861 trains ran as far west as the Missouri River. There was even talk of building a track all the way across our country to California. But many people said that was all nonsense. From the Missouri River to California was eighteen hundred long miles.

"Build a track across the plains?" the people cried. "Indians would attack! Buffaloes would block the way. What about the deserts and high mountains? You can't teach the engine to run up and down mountains!"

Lincoln listened to both sides. But he had watched the long lines of covered wagons. He had seen hundreds of men, women, and children starting west from the Missouri River bound for California. That trip would take them four or five long, hard months. Some would never get to California. There should be an easier way.

After Lincoln was made President, he signed a paper. It said that a new railroad was to be started. It was called the transcontinental railroad. *Trans* means "across." *Transcontinental* means "across the continent." Two companies were to build the road. One company was to start building west from the Missouri River. The other company was to start building east

from California. Men in New York and in San Francisco were to direct the work. When the two tracks met, the railway would be done.

There were no bulldozers in those days. There were no caterpillar tractors with derricks or cranes. Men must dig with pick and shovel. They must carry dirt in wheelbarrows. They must lift rails onto and off of wagons. The transcontinental railway must be built by hand.

Thousands of men and hundreds of teams of horses, mules, and oxen started work. Most of the men who started work at the Missouri River had come to this country from Ireland. Most of the men who started work in California came from a very different part of the world from Ireland. They spoke no English. They wore loose blue suits and straw hats tied on their heads. They had pigtails down their backs. They came from the ancient land of China.

But, Irish or Chinese, the workmen were doing something that had never been done before. They were to build a railway such as the world had never seen. They, too, were pioneers.

What was it like working on the transcontinental railroad? What was it like when, after five years of work, the last rails were laid? The next story will tell you.

The Transcontinental Railroad

Chapter 34
Building the Railroad

Mike and his father had come from Ireland. Ireland, with its green fields, was a long way off. The old country was very different from this strange, new land.

Sometimes Mike was homesick. But back in Ireland, his father's farm had been poor. The potato crop had failed, and there had been little or nothing to eat. Then his mother had died. So Mike's father had sold the farm, and little did he get for it. There was just enough money to bring the two of them to America. Now they were working on the railroad.

Mike's father was boss of his rail gang. He was a fast worker. Mike was proud of him. Mike, himself, was a water boy. He carried pails of water to the thirsty men.

Mike's hair was red. When he was excited, it stood straight up. His eyes were as blue as the lakes in Ireland. But now he was frowning, and his eyes looked dark as thunderclouds. His back ached and his hands were sore.

"I've carried enough water to float a ship!" muttered Mike.

He set his two pails down a minute to rest.

A loud, angry shout came. "Ho there, boy! Water!"

Mike grabbed his pails. A little water spilled. Mike gasped. Waste water! Water was precious in this desert land where the men were working now. Mike hurried on carefully with his pails. A man grabbed a long-handled dipper. He drank and drank. The water was stale from standing in barrels. It also was warm from the sun, but at least it was wet.

Each day, trains brought up supplies. As soon as tracks were laid, the engines began running over them. Each day the engines could go a little farther before they came to the "end of track," as the men called it. Sometimes a mile of track was laid in a day. Sometimes two miles were laid. Sometimes even more.

The trains brought up wooden ties and iron rails, spikes, and bolts. They also brought up all the food for the men and hay for the horses and mules. Now the "end of track" was in the desert, and they had to bring water as well. The water boys carried it in pails from the place where the flatcars stood.

Back and forth went Mike. The air was full of dust from the heavy wagons. The dust turned gold in the sun, but it made Mike choke and cough. The air was full of noise, as well. Wagons pounded past. Men shouted. "Clang, clang," came the sound of the hammers as the men drove in the spikes.

Suddenly there came another sound. It was right behind Mike. "Thud, thud," came the sound of hoofs. There was a shout. Mike jumped aside. He fell rolling in the dust. A big black horse went galloping by.

A boy rode on the horse's back. He was shouting at people to get out of the way. He was urging the horse on. The horse galloped down the track. Behind the horse was a long rope fastened to a rail-truck, bringing up more rails for the men at the "end of track."

Mike watched the horse. Sparks flew as its iron shoe hit a stone. Oh, how Mike longed to ride such a horse! How he longed to go galloping down the track shouting! But there was no horse for Mike. He plodded on down the path in the dust and noise with his empty pails.

Now the day's work was nearly over. No more water was needed. Mike ran over to watch his father's gang before they stopped work.

There were a few more rails to lay. The men worked fast. There were five in each gang. The men rolled a rail from the rail-truck. Three men grabbed it on one end and two men grabbed it on the other end. Quickly they slung it into its place on the wooden ties. Men with big hammers stood ready and waiting.

Then Mike's father shouted, "DOWN!"

"Clang, clang," went the hammers driving in the spikes—ten spikes to each rail, and three blows to each spike. It took just half a minute to lay a rail. Two rails a minute. The "end of track" moved forward. ❏

Chapter 35
Faster! Faster!

The two lines of track came nearer and nearer together. Now a race started between the Irish and the Chinese workers to see how much track could be laid in a day.

"Faster, faster!" went the cry.

The race was on. The men were eager and excited. The Irish worked hard to beat the Chinese. The Chinese worked equally hard to beat the Irish.

At night, the Irish told stories about those Chinese workers. Mike listened in wonder. His red hair stood on end. The Irish had done their share of hard work. They had laid the track over mountains and across the desert under the burning August sun. They had fought Indians. But the Chinese had had their share of hardship.

In the mountains, there were places where cliffs dropped straight down two thousand feet. There was no place for the tracks. A shelf must be cut in the side of the steep rock wall. The Chinese workers were let down by ropes. There they hung above the precipice. They chipped the rock away by hand. If the ropes broke they would be killed! Mike's eyes grew large as he thought of the danger.

But that was not all. The Chinese had cut tunnels through the mountains. They had blasted away the rock. But there was no dynamite in those days. Gunpowder was used to break up the rock. It was far more dangerous than dynamite. The men must light the gunpowder and then run. Sometimes they could not run fast enough.

One year, a thousand Chinese had worked in a tunnel all through the cold dark winter. It had taken two thousand men just to shovel away the snow and keep supplies coming through. The Chinese ate their rice and drank their tea, and they dug away deep in the ground.

Mike wondered about these Chinese. They were strangers. They were different. He was not sure that he liked them. He even wondered what they were like.

Once he had seen some of them driving a supply wagon. There was a boy about his own age. The Irish boys had laughed at him. They had pointed at his straw hat, his loose blue cotton clothes, and his pigtail. But the Chinese boy had paid no attention to them.

At last, news came that made every Irishman sit up.

Each day, the workers on both sides had been trying to lay a little more track than the day before. Each day, they tried to work

faster. Now came news. The Chinese had laid six miles of track in one day! Never had there been such a record.

Mike heard the men around him mutter, "We'll show them!"

Never had the work gone so quickly as it did the next day! Rail-trucks thundered along. Hammers clanged. Even Mike raced back and forth with his water buckets. He did not feel hot and tired now.

During the day, word came in. "Four miles finished. Five miles. Six miles!" Everyone cheered. They would break the record the Chinese workers had set!

Then something unexpected happened to Mike. He was hurrying along the path. A rail-truck came pounding down the track. The big black horse was galloping. It was tired and covered with foam, but the boy on his back urged him on.

Suddenly, the big animal stumbled. The boy went flying over his head. He lay on the ground. The horse stood still. By God's grace, it stopped at a spot where the track ran up a little hill, so the heavy truck came slowly to a stop.

Mike ran to the boy. He knelt beside him.

Was he badly hurt?

All at once, the boy opened his eyes. He sat up. Then he began to shout at Mike. "Get on with that load of rails!" he screamed. "Get those rails to the 'end of track'! Don't stop here."

For half a second, Mike looked at him. Then Mike grinned. His eyes flashed blue. He ran to the horse and started to climb up onto his back. It was a long way up, but Mike made it.

"Gettee-up!" shouted Mike. The horse broke into a gallop, and Mike bounced up and down. At first, he thought he would be bounced to bits, but he held on for dear life. Down the track galloped the horse with the truck behind.

The men who were waiting were angry. They did not look to see who was on the horse.

"Where have you been, boy?" shouted a red-faced man. He threw a log under the truck to stop it.

Mike had no time to explain. He pulled up his horse so fast that he went flying up onto the horse's neck. He had to grab the animal's ears to keep from going over his head. Quickly he wiggled back into place.

Then Mike's father saw who was riding the horse.

"Good work, son! Keep the rails a-coming!" his father shouted.

When the truck was empty, the men tipped it off the track. Up galloped the next horse with more rails. While Mike waited, he patted his horse's neck. He talked gently to him. The horse whinnied.

"He's tired," thought Mike, "but he likes me."

Then Mike's truck was lifted back onto the track. Down the path he went. He bounced about less now. He was getting used to the horse. Back and forth along the track he rode, confidently.

That night there was good news. Seven and a half miles of track had been laid. There were cheers and celebrations, but they did not last long.

Soon word came back from the other side. "Tomorrow we will finish ten miles in one day!" Ten miles! That was impossible!

The railway was nearly finished by now. The tracks were coming very close together. Indeed, they were so close that it was decided to give the Irish workers a holiday to go to see the fun. Ten miles of track in a day! Impossible!

Mike was up before daybreak. He rode with his father and a crowd of men in a big wagon. Across the desert, they rode. Then Mike saw the other track shining in the sunrise. It had come all the way from California to meet them.

Five long trains stood ready with rails and spikes. At seven o'clock, the signal to start work was given. Mike watched the Chinese workers hurry to their places. They were shorter than the Irish. They were slender and wiry. Then Mike's eyes opened wide. Never had he seen men work so fast! Fifteen seconds and a rail was down.

By noon, six miles were down. By seven o'clock that evening, ten miles were done! An engine ran triumphantly over the track.

The Irish went grumbling back to their own camp. The record was broken. Ten miles! And what was worse, there was nothing that they could do about it. The railroad was too nearly finished. They had only six more miles of track left to lay.

"We could have beaten them!" said Mike firmly. It did not seem fair. He foolishly became angry toward those Chinese. "We could have done eleven miles, if we'd had the chance!" ❏

Chapter 36
End of Track

There was a great celebration when the last rails were laid. Famous people came from all over the country to watch. Everyone was excited and happy.

The place where the two tracks met was in the territory of Utah, at a place called Promontory Point. It was near the Great Salt Lake. Trains came up on the tracks from both directions. They brought crowds of men in high silk hats. They brought ladies in long silk dresses and children in fine clothes. Never in his life had Mike seen such a wonderful sight.

There were people from every part of our country. Also, there were strong young men from Salt Lake City. They had helped with the grading of the land for the railway. There were African Americans and Mexicans, for some of them, too, had been working. Irish and Chinese swarmed everywhere. A few tall, silent Indians sat on their horses and watched.

At last, everything was ready. Two engines stood facing each other. Then the last pair of rails was laid between them. A band played. There were speeches. Then a gentleman lifted a big hammer. He drove in the last spike in the transcontinental railroad. That spike was made of pure gold!

The two engines steamed forward until they touched. The people clapped and shouted and threw their caps into the air. The whistles on the engines blew until Mike thought his ears would burst. Bells began to ring, and men fired their guns into the air. The horses were frightened. Mules brayed. Then the band began to play so loud that you could not hear your own voice.

Mike was screaming as loud as anyone. He was jumping up and down. Suddenly, he saw that he was standing beside a Chinese boy. Mike forgot that he did not like Chinese people. Before he knew it, the two boys were clapping each other on the back. They were laughing and shouting and shaking hands. Then they turned cartwheels and tumbled over on the ground.

Mike's hair shone red in the sun. His eyes were as blue as the sky. The Chinese boy's dark eyes shone with excitement and joy. The two could not talk together, but they grinned. They started laughing and shouting all over again.

Then a procession formed in back of the band. The two boys ran after it. They were no longer two strangers from two very different lands. Side by side they marched. They had both worked on the great transcontinental railroad. They were both Americans, and they both honored hard work.

Abraham Lincoln did not live to see the railroad finished. The President had been shot by a foolish man who hated him. The country mourned his loss. But, as he had hoped, the new railway did help to unite the East and the West into one United States of America. The first transcontinental railroad line was completed on May 10, 1869.

And so, little by little, our country changed from a land of covered wagons and homespun cloth and log cabins to a land of railways and factories and machinery. But it is not engines and factories that make a country great. There are no factories to make men like George Washington. There are no machines to make children brave and strong and kind. Only the Spirit of God and God's Word can make a soul truly great.

The people who live in a country make it great. A country is great if its people are brave and honest and unselfish. A country is great if its people can work together for the glory of Jesus Christ.

Pioneer children from every land helped to make our country what it is. Children of today are just as important. They can help find new and better ways of doing things. They, too, can be pioneers and let the holy light of truth shine through their lives to light up a world made dark by sin. ❏

1. First, the men went to find the best route. They fought storms and Indians. They climbed mountains.

Building The Transcontinental Railroad

2. Next came the graders who made the roadbed smooth and even. They dug away hills. They filled in low places.

3. Wooden bridges or trestles were built over deep canyons. There were plenty of great pine trees in the forests.

4. Next came the men to lay the wooden ties for the tracks to rest upon. Around four million ties were needed.

5. Last of all came the T-rails. These rails were brought up in a rail-truck—four hundred rails to the mile.

6. Down went a pair of rails. A man measured to see that they were the right distance apart.

7. Then down swung the big hammers—ten spikes to a rail, and three blows to a spike. Twelve thousand blows every mile.

8. Sometimes Indians attacked while the men were working. They dropped their tools and picked up the guns they kept close by.

Questions

1. In what year did Abraham Lincoln become president?

2. What does the word *Transcontinental* mean?

3. How many miles of railroad track would be needed to go from the Missouri River to California?

4. How many years did it take to build the first transcontinental railroad line?

5. Why were the Irish workers upset when the last rails were put into place?

6. When was the first transcontinental railroad line completed?

Things to Do

1. Go to the library and find a picture book that shows you how railroad bridges were built in the late 1800's. Build a railroad bridge out of popsicle sticks and glue.

2. Draw a picture of an old-fashioned railroad locomotive.

3. Visit a railroad museum with your parents or some other adult. If you do not have a museum in your area, visit a local hobby shop and study the model trains that they have available.

4. Put together a model of a miniature plastic train car or locomotive.

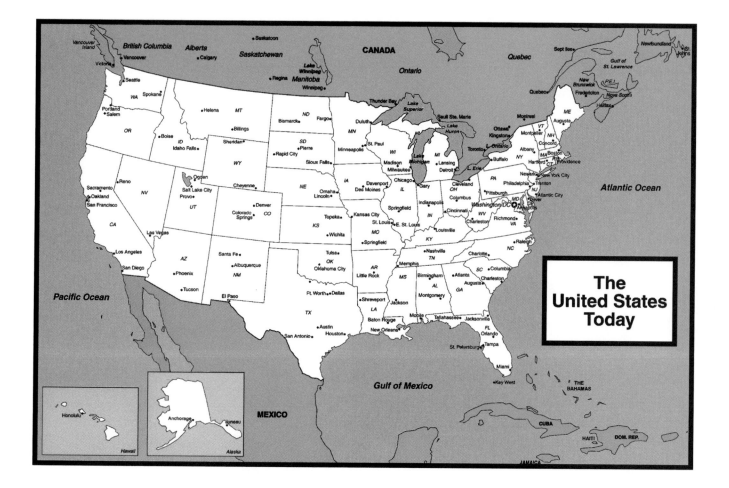